Annah Maud Gould

From the author's collection.

Cover: the *Berlin*

Courtesy of the Maine Maritime Museum

A TEMPESTUOUS VOYAGE

The Diary of Annah Maud Gould's Trip
Aboard the Ship *Berlin*

Edited By
Laura Penny

HERITAGE BOOKS, INC.
1987

Published By
HERITAGE BOOKS, INC.
3602 Maureen Lane, Bowie, MD 20715

ISBN 1-55613-030-9

PROLOGUE

On January 16, 1887, the ship *Berlin* sailed from the port of Philadelphia bound for San Francisco. Along with Captain Frank D. Whitmore and crew, the *Berlin* carried the captain's wife, Mrs. Mary Palmer Whitmore, and their son, Morton P. Whitmore, and the Misses Annah Maud Gould and Julia M. Folsom. Captain Whitmore anticipated a voyage of approximately four months, arriving in San Francisco by way of Cape Horn sometime in early May. The *Berlin*, however, did not dock in California until September 5, 1887, nearly eight months after embarking upon her voyage.

Throughout the lengthy journey, Maud Gould kept a diary of life aboard the *Berlin*, chronicling not only day-to-day happenings but also the more unusual occurances. Maud's account of the voyage is detailed and needs little clarification but I have taken the liberty of adding some background information to fill in historical details. No changes have been made in Maud's text other than punctuation and spelling corrections. The log is, as Maud writes, "a faithful report of a woman's life on board ship" and it is presented as such.

INTRODUCTION

Maud Gould was an adventurous woman. In 1887, at the age of thirty one, she undertook a sea voyage of many thousands of miles, traveling from Philadelphia to San Francisco by way of Cape Horn. Few women, other than captain's wives, made this long hard journey, even fewer were "maiden ladies" as were Maud and her traveling companion, Julia M. Folsom.

Annah Maud Gould was born March 19, 1855 in New Sharon, Maine, daughter of Oliver and Mary Ballard (Crowell) Gould. The Goulds lived in New Sharon when Maud was a child, moving to Augusta, Maine when she was in her teens. After her father's death in 1873, Maud continued to live in Augusta with her mother. Not much is known of Maud's personal life, except that she never married and, with the exception of her log, none of her correspondence with family or friends exists today. Maud's personality shows in her writing; she had a flair for detailed descriptions and a dry sense of humor which is apparent throughout her log.

Maud died February 11, 1899 at the age of forty three; the exact place of her death is unknown. Family records say she died in Santa Barbara, California but California has no record of her death. Maine records, likewise, provide no information on her death. She is buried in the Gould family plot in the Mt. Pleasant Cemetery in Augusta, Maine.

Maud was influenced in her style of writing by the log of a similar voyage made by Morton McMichael (*A Landlubber's Log*, published 1883). Maud found that, once on board ship, she could not do many of the things described by Mr. McMichael in his log. She was not free to visit the carpenter's shop when she so desired; she could not talk freely to the ship's crew or mates; nor could she climb the rigging without causing shipwide commotion. The limitations surrounding a woman's life on land were even greater on board ship and Maud realized a woman's report of shipboard life would be less exciting than a man's. That, however, did not stop her from keeping her log and carefully chronicling life on board the *Berlin*.

Maud's log also includes descriptions of the other people on board the *Berlin*. Maud's traveling companion was Julia Morse Folsom, daughter of David and Rachel (Abbott) Folsom. Julia was born about 1853 in Augusta, Maine and died in Augusta December 28, 1905. According to Maud, Julia also kept an account of the *Berlin*'s voyage. A search for this journal was unsuccessful, an unfortunate circumstance because a comparison of Julia's account and Maud's account of the voyage would provide a more complete picture of life on board the ship.

Captain and Mrs. Whitmore are mentioned often in the log. Captain Franklin Delano Whitmore was born May 9, 1839 in Arrowsic, Maine, son of William C. and Phebe (Hayden) Whitmore. Frank began his sailing career as a common sailor at the age of sixteen, eventually becoming a master mariner. He commanded the *Thomas M. Lord*, the *Alice M. Minott* for seven years, the *Berlin* for nine years, and the *Mary Russell*. In 1897 Captain Whitmore broke his leg on board ship in the China Sea during a typhoon and had to give up sailing. He died March 23, 1900 in Gardiner, Maine.

Mrs. Whitmore, the former Mary Noyes Palmer, was born May 23, 1851 in Gardiner, Maine. She was the daughter of William and Anna Maria (Noyes) Palmer. Mary Palmer and Frank Whitmore were married August 12, 1871 in Gardiner.

The Whitmore's had three children, Mary Lilli, Frank H., and Morton P. The youngest child, Morton P., was also on the 1887 voyage of the *Berlin* He is described in detail by Maud in her log. Morton must have made the long journey more interesting for the others since the antics of a one-year-old would keep everyone entertained.

Maud looked upon the Whitmores and Julia as her family. Living in such close contact with the others must have been difficult at times yet there seemed to be few personality conflicts. They depended upon one another for entertainment, help when they were ill, and moral support when the journey seemed to last forever. No doubt these friendships lasted well beyond the day the *Berlin* docked in San Francisco.

THE *BERLIN*

The ship *Berlin* was built at the C. V. Minott shipyard in Phippsburg, Maine. Launched in October 1882, she was built of wood, weighed one thousand six hundred thirty four tons, had a beam width of forty feet, a depth of twenty four feet and a total length of two hundred twenty two and one half feet.

The *Berlin* was a type of ship known as a down-easter. The development of the down-easter occurred for various reasons. In the years after the Civil War the demand for traditional sailing freighters declined. Use of steamships was growing on the shorter coastal routes where cheap coal supplies were available but these steamships could not undertake the long journeys around Cape Horn because the expense and difficulty of buying coal in foreign ports was prohibitive. Trade with the Pacific Coast was growing rapidly and the need to transport goods from east coast to west coast became essential. As the products produced by California's ranches, farms, and vineyards, and the lumber from Washington and Oregon became more important to the eastern United States, a new coast-to-coast trade rose to meet the new demands. This trade, with California grain as the primary cargo, was the main factor in the growing demand for wooden sailing ships.

The famous clipper ships of the 1850s and 1860s were adapted to carry the California grain cargos. The clippers were fast ships, built for speed, not for carrying large, bulky cargos. Owners soon found that the clippers were not economically sound investments for the Cape Horn trade. The clipper required a large crew to maintain her on a voyage, costing the owners more money than they felt necessary. Shipbuilders soon began to realize that speed was not as important in shipping California grain as was having a sound, sturdy, reliable ship that was cost-effective.

The type of ship the owners demanded was a deep-sea square rigged ship, of medium size and great power with good speed. These ships had to be built tightly and strongly because grain was a perishable cargo and it must be shipped in good condition. The ships were to be economical, using only one half the crew of a clipper.

The type of ship the owners were demanding was nothing new. It was the sort of ship the shipbuilders of Maine had been constructing and launching for many years. These sturdy ships became known as down easters because they were built Down East in ports such as Bath, Phippsburg, and Thomaston, Maine. A few of the down-easters were also built in Newburyport, Massachusetts; Portsmouth, New Hampshire; and Mystic and Stonington, Connecticut. Under the leadership of the builders in Bath, Maine, they continued to build bigger and better ships for deep-sea trade. During the 1870s and 1880s, Maine built the most profitable and most economic merchant fleet ever.

Down-easters were often referred to as "tubs" and "slowpokes" by the builders of New York and Boston. The down-easter was slow compared to the clipper and had only a very moderate sail spread. The down-easters, however, made money steadily, made fair passage round the Cape, were excellent deep sea ships, and delivered cargo in better condition than had the clippers. Down-easters had a good cargo carrying capacity and made fairly good speed; they were seaworthy, strong, reasonably easy to operate and maintain and called for a small crew. The down-easter continued to sail long after the clipper ships had discontinued their service.

During the heyday of the down-easters, New York and Boston almost stopped building wooden ships altogether. The shipyards of New England and especially Maine made up for that stoppage. By 1875, Maine shipyards were constructing approximately eighty per cent of the square-rigged vessels built in the United States. During the peak years of construction, 1881-1885, shipyards such as Sewall and Houghton of Bath, Thompson of Kennebunk, Pascal of Camden, and Reed and Minott of Phippsburg were launching a total average of thirty two ships per year.

The ships were generally managed by brokers in New York or Boston with the shares of the ship owned by the builder, captain, private investors or various others. Often a ship was built specifically for an individual captain. A ship was usually named after her largest shareholder, most often this would be the builder but sometimes the name might be that of someone not involved in the actual construction of the ship.

The cost of running an average down-easter was close to $25,000 per year. The dividends paid to the owners/investors were approximately fifteen to twenty per cent per year.

The Cape Horn passage was the most difficult passage a ship could make. The builders knew this and built vessels that could withstand the rigors of the passage. Sails, ropes and all equipment were of the best quality and were replaced at the first sign of wear. Everything from the hull to the furnishings on a down-easter were of the finest quality of workmanship, built to last many years. The ships making the trip round the Horn carried such low-grade cargos as coffee, hides, jute, case oil, sugar, wool, and coal. The primary money-making cargo was grain from California, shipped to the East Coast and European ports such as Liverpool. The down-easters had low overhead costs and because they had no need of fuel supplies, they were an economical way to carry the cargos from port to port.

The greatest years for sailing vessels such as the down-easter were the 1880s. Between the years 1880-1886, more than one hundred American ships were used each year to transport goods from coast to coast. During a four year period ending 30 June 1885, 1,521 sailing vessels left San Francisco carrying grain. The down-easter, in her many years of service, provided an economical way to move cargo from port to port and helped Maine hold her place in the business of shipbuilding.

The *Berlin* sailed in the Cape Horn and Far East case oil trades until 1890 when she was sold to G. E. Plummer of San Francisco. Plummer used the *Berlin* in the west coast coal trade for seven years, selling her in 1897 to the Alaska-Portland Packers Association for use in shipping goods to the Alaskan salmon canneries. The *Berlin* sailed in the fleet of the Alaska-Portland Packers for fifteen years. She made annual voyages to Nushagak (Alaska) to take cannery workers and supplies north and returned to Portland in the fall with the cannery crews and a portion of the salmon pack.

On May 19, 1922, the *Berlin* was bound for Nushagak when she was stranded on an open beach at Ugaguk, forty miles from her destination. No lives were lost in the wreck; the two hundred cannery workers and crew of seventeen were landed safely. The *Berlin* carried a cargo of lumber, tinplate, labels, and cans intended for the salmon pack. The cargo was rendered useless and unsalvagable because of salt water damage.

ix

The mast of the *Berlin* were cut away to give the wreck buoyancy and she was hauled into shallow waters for salvaging. The wireless radio was moved on shore so communications were possible with the Alaska-Portland Packers plant at Nushagak and daily progress messages were routed to the Portland office.

The *Berlin's* career as a cargo ship ended on the beach in Alaska. She was forty years old when she went down. Her peak years of service had been in the 1880s and Maud's diary captures the heyday of the *Berlin* and the down-easter.

NEWSPAPER EXCERPTS

Daily Alta California (San Francisco, CA)
6 September 1887

A Tempestuous Voyage
Three Ladies Take a Pleasure Trip of 231 Days at Sea

The American ship *Berlin* arrived in port last evening after a tempestuous voyage of 231 days from Philadelphia. On January 17th last the vessel left the Breakwater carrying, in addition to a heavy cargo and a full crew, the captain's wife, Mrs. F. D. Whitemore, and two young lady passengers, Miss Maud Sewall and Miss Julia M. Folsom, of Augusta, Me. After being out three days the mate met with injuries sufficiently severe to cause Captain Whitemore to return to port, where the injured man could be better cared for. Strong gales were encountered until February 15th, on which date the *Berlin* crossed the Atlantic equator in longitude 26 degrees 52 minutes west. Exceedingly light and variable winds were as far south as 50 degrees where, on March 19th, the vessel encountered a gale off Cape Horn. She beat about for several days, the cargo shifting and the ship losing several spars and sails.

Port Stanley, Falkland Islands, was reached in safety, Captain Whitemore discharging and restowing cargo, and making other needed repairs. While in port the crew became mutinous and refused to work. Not wishing to experience trouble at sea with the ladies in his care the master promptly discharged the men and shipped a new crew from Valparaiso. After leaving Port Stanley heavy weather was again experienced until July 30th, when the *Berlin* crossed the equator at 120 degrees west longitude.

Mrs. Whitemore and the Misses Sewall and Folsom were called upon last night at their apartment at the Lick by an

Alta reporter. They expressed themselves as being delighted with their trip, but they nevertheless appeared equally delighted to be ashore. Captain Whitemore will to-day prefer charges of insubordination against five members of his crew.

Why Maud is referred to as Maud Sewall is unknown. She had Sewall cousins and Julia also had Sewall cousins. Perhaps it was a mistake made by the reporter.

Daily Kennebec Journal (Augusta, ME)
7 September 1887

Considerable anxiety has been felt for the last few months by the friends of Miss Maud Gould and Miss Julia Folsom of this city regarding their safety. It will be remembered that they sailed for San Francisco from Philadelphia, January 16th on the ship *Berlin* commanded by Capt. Whitmore of Gardiner. When next heard from they were at the Falkland Islands where they remained eight weeks. Since that time nothing has been heard from them until yesterday when the anxiety of their friends was relieved by the following dispatch:

San Francisco, Cal., Sept. 5.
Mrs. M. B. Gould:
Anchored safely in San Francisco Harbor. All well.
                    Maud Gould

A LOG:

BEING THE FAITHFUL RECORD OF
A TRIP ROUND CAPE HORN

AS UNDERTAKEN BY A MISGUIDED DAMSEL
IN SEARCH OF "FUN."

PREFACE

In these days of much writing there must be a preface and introduction to every sketch of whatever length and whatever degree of unworldliness, wherein is described the end, aim, and object of the author's efforts; consequently my little record must possess a preface. Its aim and object being to announce to the very elect number of its readers that it had been throughout my intention to follow carefully in the footsteps of Mr. Morton McMichael, who made this same voyage and whose little book entitled *A Landlubber's Log*, did much to influence me in a final decision to take this trip. But I had hardly landed a day on board ship before I discovered that the limitations, necessarily surrounding a woman's life, were in no wise lessened at sea, in fact no where were the bounds to be more carefully recognized.

For instance, some of Mr. McMichael's more racy chapters were devoted to descriptions of interviews held by him with the second mate and even some of the other men, while some of his happiest hours were passed in the carpenter's shop gossiping with "Chips." To our second mate I did speak for weeks, and at all times and seasons our conversation has been strictly limited to passing the time of day and the shortest of commonplaces, as to addressing a sailor or even noticing one unless absolutely necessary I should as soon think of embracing a stranger upon the street. I have paid one or two short visits to the carpenter, but his shop being decidedly in the forbidden district I went under the powerful escort of the Captain.

As for taking my exercise running up and down the rigging, keeping a lookout for ships and whales at the mast-heads, or spending whole forenoons on the main royal yards, these, I feared, were little feats that might become a young and sprightly youth; but my own feeble attempt in that direction, a visit to the mizzenmast head, modestly paid at twilight with the Captain to sustain and direct my faltering steps and with Mr. Dow stationed below prepared to leap overboard if I should

1

happen to take a header sea-ward, my one attempt, I say, quite makes me blush when I think how the report of it, exaggerated and enlarged upon may come back to me after a brisk circulation among the ship.

In consequence of these slight drawbacks to my acceptance of Mr. McM. as a model, I have come to the conclusion that, in keeping a log, I must follow my own plan and be my own model, and although a faithful report of woman's life on board ship may be far less exciting that that of a man's, still, if carefully made, it may be of interest to a few friends or to those to whom this life is new.

INTRODUCTION

When about to set out from Philadelphia for San Francisco via Cape Horn, I planned to keep a log. It certainly did not form part of my plans that my first entry in that log should be made February 27, nearly six weeks from the time of sailing. But it was even so and Alas! for my vain glorifying, of my boasting of immunity from sea-sickness, for three long weeks, miserable weeks, the dreaded mal-de-mer held me in its pitiless grasp, the proverbial "inch of hell" being lengthened to yards in my case. However my sufferings never forced me to confess that I was sorry I came or that the attacks of sea-sickness were worse than attacks of nausea from which I suffer at home, only being more frequent and of longer duration. I was much weakened, consequently I was a long time recovering and even after I was seemingly quite strong my eyes were troublesome and I was unable to read or write much. My impressions of the first part of the voyage, that from Philadelphia nearly to the Equator, being very vague and mostly hearsay, I have therefore decided to make no entries of that time, beyond useful general statements as to our luck in getting on or the manner passing our time, but instead give a careful description of the ship itself and of the mode and manner of life of its different occupants as now in the light of longer experience I am able to do.

January 6

Behold us there on a cold, dark, stormy January morning setting out upon a way decidedly new and untried. We left Augusta at the unearthly hour of six a.m. that we might reach Philadelphia Friday night as the ship was to sail on Saturday. I say was to sail, but the Fates forbad and for eight long days we lay at the wharf expecting every day to sail and every day the cold grew more intense and the ice on the river thicker until our hearts were heavy within us and almost we wished we had not entered upon such an undertaking. Although surrounded by friends we could not get leave to be away from the ship longer that a few hours for fear we might not be at hand when the orders came for her to sail.

However all things good or bad have an ending and on Sunday, January 16 at five a.m. the tug and ice-boats came along side, the sailors tumbled aboard and with much noise and confusion we were finally off. Sunday we spent in writing letters to send back by the pilot, in the stowing away and making fast all moveable objects, walking on the house and remaining on deck to gaze upon places of interest as we slowly steamed down the river.

At four p.m. the ice-boats left us and six p.m. found us anchored off Capes Henlopen and May at the mouth of the Delaware River. Here we remained all day Monday as there was a heavy head wind blowing thirty or forty [m.p.h.], other vessels keeping us company. At five in the afternoon the wind changed and the Captain ordered all sails set and we, the only venturesome one of the fleet, started out upon our fifteen thousand mile journey, darkness before us, dark clouds over our heads and a wind that was almost a hurricane our propelling force.

Julia and I were ignominiously sent to bed by Mrs. Whitmore before the anchors were up. Although we were allowed to partake of some light refreshment after we were comfortably settled, I appeared at breakfast next morning but I did not tarry long, and over the next two weeks I kindly draw a

5

veil.

Not that I suffered anguish the whole time for on Friday of that week I was lying out on deck clothed in thin garments for we were already in warm weather. I enjoyed the warmth and brightness but my appetite was not of quixotic proportions and I still suffered from the effects of an illness which visited me in Philadelphia. Still, I think I should have done very well if a fresh breeze had not sprung up and, in conjunction with a contrary and high sea, produced a motion most fitly designated the "cork screw" motion. The sensation is incredible, but it is warranted to produce an attack of sea-sickness surpassing in violence anything ever suffered before. My second condition was so much worse than my first that I quite despaired and I think both Captain and Mrs. Whitmore were anxious. Both were most kind, Mrs. Whitmore especially, arranging her bed for my occupancy during the day as it had a spring and was most comfortable, and in preparing little articles of food to benefit my appetite which still lingered. Indeed it seemed to me at times that I never could go to the table again for the rattle of the dishes nauseated me. They very kindly did not urge me but sent my meals to me day after day and, after the Captain had ordered my hammock strung on deck, I often had my noon-day meal served there, but suddenly and without warning I felt better, my appetite returned and after a while my strength came to me and I was as a new woman.

During this time we had not been at a standstill; for days we had strong, favorable winds, one day making two hundred seventy odd miles, thus breaking the *Berlin*'s past record by several miles. I heard rumors of our doings and whereabouts, portions occasionally from the *North Atlantic Sailing Directions* and much talk of running far to the eastward. We passed the Tropic of Cancer without being becalmed, a wonderful bit of luck, as it is notoriously a calm belt. The name "horse latitude" has been given it because so many horses were sacrificed there in past times in order that the food and water might suffice to maintain the remaining few until a port could be reached. Also the "Sargasso Sea," a sea of weeds, was entered upon and passed safely through. This sea was merely a calm spot surrounded by currents, itself being motionless, it does not lose any of the sea-weeds or mosses collected by the different currents and deposited in its waters.

The Equator, our first goal, as marking the first section of our journey was reached in twenty eight days, thus leaving three days to devote to the Cape if necessary, as we were allowed a month in which to make the Equator.

After passing the Equator the ill-luck that attended in Philadelphia, but since then had seemed to desert us, visited us once more and now came to stay. The part of the South American coast designated Cape Il Roque gives sea-faring people much trouble, for if a ship gets jammed north of it, she may tack about for weeks before getting clear of the land, even if she be not wrecked, for she runs a double danger having the land on one side and a cruel ledge of rocks, called the Rocas, on the other. On the latter many a good ship has come to grief. The Rocas is an island of coral formation, the only one of the kind in the Atlantic, lying in Latitude three degrees fifty seven minutes and Longitude thirty two degrees twenty four minutes W., eighty four miles west of Fernando Noronha (a Brazilian convict station), ninety miles north of Cape Il Roque and three hundred miles to the eastward. Owing to its being wrongly located on the charts it has proved to be a ship trap for years. As its highest point it is not more than ten feet above the surface of the water, it is not discovered until the unlucky vessel is right upon it and a strong easterly current helps to drive the ship to its destruction. There is a lagoon of beautiful clear water in the center.

We had made such an extraordinary run to eastward (most easterly point being twenty four degrees twenty five minutes W.) passing the Equator in twenty seven degrees W. that the Captain had no fears of coming in contact with the Cape. The course for a ship sailing from NY or Philadelphia in south, east, south-east, which is almost a diagonal run across the Atlantic, the extreme limit of easting must be determined by the season of the year, for the limits of the trade winds vary considerably for the different months of the year but the variation is carefully set down in the sailing directions, so there is no difficulty in knowing the exact degree in which to take the desired trade. Our S.E. trade instead of being E.S.E. was S. by E. and continued in that direction for three days and the consequence was that in nine degrees S. we found ourselves only a few miles from the coast and decidedly jammed there. Land was sighted at about three p.m. and at six we tacked ship, all hands mustering on deck to witness the feat, it being the first time since we came out and consequently was quite new to Julia and myself.

The first sight of land, after weeks of sea and one's first experience of sea too, is a delectable sight, I could have embraced the low-lying mounds looking so dim and hazy in the distance.

February 18

The next morning early we took a tack landward and at ten a.m. when I appeared on deck such a beautiful view was spread out before me. We were so near we could distinguish between sand and grassland on the succession of mounds lying in a long line to west-ward, the time being summer there was only a faint tinge of green, the prevailing color being a delicate pinkish tint evidently due to coloring of the earth or sand. Instead of chalky we had pinkish cliffs and through the glass we could see the surf break along the beach. The Captain was anxious to locate the exact position on the coast so we studied the *South Atlantic Sailing Directions* for landmarks and spent hours in persuading ourselves that two innocent rocks were the steeple of a church, a line of darkish color in the cliffs was a light-house and a least two dozen palm trees, as they opened up, were declared to be two particular palms said to serve as guides for ships approaching the coast. To add to our excitement small sails were seen, through the glass, fluttering about and one was observed to set out from what we thought to be a settlement and make directly for us; the craft sporting these sails were pronounced to be catamarans extensively employed be the fishermen on this coast. We ardently hoped that the one bearing down upon us was coming for the purpose of trade and made up our minds to dine upon fish with a dessert of fresh fruit and coconuts, as the Captain said these men frequently boarded ships to barter these delicacies for tobacco or clothing. But Alas! for our expectations that catamaran most anxiously watched proved delusive as its fellows and after a little tacked about and followed its companions to the fishing grounds, I suppose, as after reaching a certain point they all remained stationery, we could count eight or nine sails in the group.

That evening our zeal in discovering landmarks reached the culminating point, we were exactly in the track of the coast trading vessels, therefore a sharp lookout must be kept seaward, and the land carefully scanned for light-houses which would establish our exact whereabouts; of course the Captain knew at what latitude the lights were but he could not tell just how much we had made since taking the last sight, for we had been tacking about all afternoon. Consequently he assembled the family on deck armed with glasses of all descriptions, stationed a man aloft and was constantly ordering the officer on deck to run up the mast-head for a sight. A person who has never tried can have an idea how anxiety aided by a powerful imagination leads one to discover lights on all

8

sides. The Captain and Julia must have been of the most imaginative turn of mind, for out of the reflected light of a sugar refinery they made a first-class revolving light, flashing red and white alternately, laboriously counting one--two--three, up to sixty to prove that the flashes followed each other within an interval of a moment.

Loud were the railings and deep their disgust when more lights appeared and, at last, four or five factories or refineries were seen in full blast and as darkness deepened they finely illumined the western sky. The expected light-house did not put in an appearance until midnight, it being further south than we at first supposed.

We were constantly passing vessels or steamers, the latter always distinguishable by the bright white lights at the mast-head. The discovery of a red light on our starboard side caused a great commotion and peremptory order from the Captain for the men at the wheel to put the tiller down, that the ship might be put about. The excitement was over in five minutes but the danger lay in the fact that both ships were on the wind and the two courses crossed each other diagonally, that is the one would pass across the bows of the other and as it is impossible to estimate at what rate of speed each vessel is sailing one cannot tell whether they will pass each other safely or collide, but the chances are that they will collide, unless there is quick work, which we made, for by staying our course two minutes the stranger passed our bows and we saw her red light on our port-side, for "green to green or red to red is perfect safety, go ahead."

As we saw the red light it was our duty to keep away from it, if we had seen their green light from our port side, then they would have seen our green light, we should have gone on and they would have changed their course. It is only by a careful and immediate observance of these laws that collisions are avoided. As it is, the Captain says there are scores of accidents owing to a failure on the part of the officers to act quickly. A month later almost in the same latitude, under almost the same circumstances, a large emmigrant ship was run into and sunk and many lives lost.

At about this time the Southern Cross appeared low down in the horizon of the southern sky, and night after night the brilliant and diversified coloring of the evening sky feasted our eyes and delighted our hearts. One combination of slender crescent moon, brilliant evening star directly beneath and very near with a background of clear, cloudless sky of the most ravishing pink, blue, and gray tints I particularly remember.

About this time too, we received nightly visits of not the

most agreeable description, the visitor being a big black bird called by the sailors the "booby." Imagine a bird as large as a crow, with the general appearance of a bat and with the bat's propensity to swoop down upon defenseless people sitting about, and you have the booby.

In the center of the forward cabin is the dining table with a long bench or settee on either side, the port bench Julia and I share, the one on the opposite side Mrs. Whitmore occupies, while the two ends are devoted to the Captain and the baby, the Captain in an armchair at my right and the baby in a high chair at Julia's left, that is, when he is allowed to appear at the table at all for he is just at the clutching age and even with Axel stationed at the back of his chair, he manages to make articles, within his reach, fly about in a most lively manner.

Between the doors leading outside there is a deep alcove lined with zinc within which the large coal stove is firmly anchored. On either side of the cabin and opposite are doors leading repectively into the steward's pantry and store room. Just beyond the store room and opening from this cabin is Julia's stateroom.

On the end of the cabin opposite that leading to the deck are two doors leading to the after cabin, or sitting room or general gathering place. On either side in two shallow alcoves there are two sofas. Two large easy chairs occupy either end of the cabin or positions on either side of a small library table, which, as the weather permits, is placed in a commanding position in the center of the room, or forced to withdraw to a safer but less prominent abiding place in front of one of the sofas. The danger attending the position in the center of the room is due to the fact that the room is lighted by a sky-light and in bad weather, water is liable to descend in showers from the sky-light. If heavy seas are shipped unawares, or when the shutters are not up, and this happened in the evening, the lighted lamp, which is lashed to the table, might suffer from the drenching. Opening from the after cabin are my stateroom and Mrs. Whitmore's room on one side and the Captain's office and bath-room on the other. Mrs. Whitmore's room is a very elegant apartment indeed, rather larger than the cabin. It contains a large standard bed which with so many berths about, looks particularly homelike and comfortable. Besides the bed there is a large marble-topped dressing case, a sofa, wardrobe, and the baby's crib, also four good sized windows. The companion-way has, besides the outside doors, doors leading to the after cabin, Mrs. Whitmore's room, and the wash-room. The last mentioned room contains a set basin, and the medicine and book cases, very elegant affairs in black walnut and glass, with a case of four drawers under each.

The wood used in finishing both cabins is of the most beautiful description, some of it being the California cedar; several varieties are used and are highly polished and beautifully veined. It is lovely to look at but I must say I pined for plain dark wood in rough weather for the slightest scratch shows and it is almost impossible, when the ship is rolling heavily, not to bang or bring up heavily against some portion of this wall, in making one's way about the room. I deemed myself very fortunate in not leaving my mark on either cabin, until one day, not in rough weather either, the slop-pail and I lurched heavily against the door leading from the forward to after cabin and it is needless to say we left our mark.

Stepping from the companion-way to the deck we face the wheel-house, a much smaller edifice than either of the other houses, with a wide bit of deck on either side and a very narrow bit behind it and between it and the rail extending about the stern of the ship. About this wheel-house we sit and lounge and live our out-of-door life. We have an awning spread on one side and under it our hammocks are hung and our chairs are placed. At night the awning is taken down and we enjoy the sunsets, the moonlight, the stars, and the boobies. The roof or the top of the whole after-house furnishes us with space for our evening promenade. In exercising there we have employment for both mind and body, for mind in estimating the number of feet walked and reducing them, when found, to some portion of a mile, and in bad weather comparing the amount of strength expended in keeping one's balance in walking short distances, with the amount expended in walking much longer distances.

Our family is limited to the occupants of the after cabin; it is customary for the first mate to take his meals with the family, but this voyage the Captain thought it would be more agreeable and convenient to be by ourselves. More agreeable because there are always two tables, the second mate and carpenter taking their meals after the Captain and first officer and of course there could be no lingering at the first table, for when it is the second officer's watch below, he naturally desires to lose no time, but to return to his berth promptly at eight a.m. More convenient, for the first breakfast is served at seven and that would necessitate our rising at the unearthly hour of half-past six. As it is Julia and I hear the first bell

11

and the second and need not stir until the clatter of knives and forks is stilled and we know that the second breakfast has been served and devoured and then, as the steward is slow, with quick work we are ready for breakfast at quarter past eight. Our dinner is at one, supper at six p.m.

Supper is the favorite meal with us all, whether because the arduous duties of the day being over we are prepared to enjoy ourselves, or whether our appetites are sharpened by the long day in bracing air or, perhaps, as we all think, it is because the steward had more time to devote to the concoction of tasty little dishes. Be it as it may, we certainly enjoy that meal far more than either of the others.

The breakfast for me is rather a farce, for not drinking coffee and having no milk and that most of the time lukewarm and only condensed for the oatmeal, I sometimes find it difficult to make a pretense of eating, especially after the potatoes left us.

For dinner we always have a most excellent soup for the first course, either pea, tomato, vegetable, barley or some of the fancy soups put up in cans. On Tuesdays and Fridays we are favored with baked beans, canned meat of some kind being always served with this popular sea-dish; on Thursdays tinned roast beef; on Saturdays salt-fish, prepared much more daintily than I ever ate it elsewhere; on Wednesday tinned salmon; on Mondays a boiled dinner. We have every variety of canned fruit and vegetables, our California peaches and English marmalade being the favorite dessert and tomatoes the favorite vegetable. On Sunday we have especially elaborate meals, fish balls for breakfast, chicken for dinner and the famous plum duff for dessert, the batter being the most indigestible compound in existence. For supper we have lobster salad, sardines, hot rolls, tarts, cookies, and etc., in fact so many good things that we are rather over-powered. Every thing in England or America that can be bought in cans we had on board and it was really surprising that we could have such a variety even after being out eight months.

So much has and will continue to be said of Captain and Mrs. Whitmore in this log that it hardly seems necessary to enter into a very minute description but a few remarks on their personal appearance may not be out of place. The Captain is not at all a typical sea-man or old salt; he is of medium height, rather inclined to stoop, brown-haired, brown whiskers and mustache, very gentlemanly in appearance and manner. Always well and carefully dressed, boots as brightly blacked as if he were going to business every morning in the city, exquisitely neat, particular and orderly in all his habits, in every way a desirable man to have about the house, except when his usually serene disposition has been unbearably tried by a long succession of head winds or calms. On such occasions he tries to occupy his mind by putting some locker or drawer in order, or has the carpenter to perform some imaginary bit of repairing. He would enjoy having every member of the family running about waiting upon him. However, we occasionally strike for we consider that he is rather too fond of keeping us employed and needs a lesson once in a while. But as he is quite ready to run about for us, dray us about the decks in bad weather, hang hammocks in fine, and act as escort in all matters we do not often rebel.

Mrs. Whitmore may truly be called a fine specimen of robust and perfectly healthy womanhood. She is as tall as I and weighs one hundred and eighty pounds, thirty of which I must say I envy her, she is fair-haired and blue-eyed and says in foreign countries she is often asked is she not of German nationality; she has not quite an American look. She is devoted to the Captain and although she hates going to sea, having been constantly for nearly sixteen years, she can't make up her mind to say decidedly that she will go no longer.

On the one occasion of her going home intending to remain a year, the Captain telegraphed her from Russia that he was sick and to come to him at once, so leaving one child in Gardiner and with a baby a year and a half old she made the out-of-her-way spot in northern Russia, not knowing in what condition she might find her husband; imagine her disgust when he met her as brisk and well as usual and much more fleshy than when she saw him last. The mate told her that the Captain had been humming "I need thee every hour" the whole passage.

The baby is a dear little fellow, he was ten months old when we left Philadelphia and from being a pale, hollow-eyed, sober, quiet baby, he has developed into a stout, hearty, brown-faced boy, full of frolic and fun; he is our unfailing source of amusement. He is constantly learning and taking up by himself little new tricks and ways with which to enchant us.

Julia and myself make up the family circle.

Our immediate attendants are the steward and Axel, the Swedish cabin boy. The steward and cook are celestial brethren, both sporting cues. The steward's bobbed gracefully at the top of his head and with bangs all round so that with his cap on his cue is entirely hidden and he appears to wear his

13

hair short. The cook confines himself so closely to his own quarters that we have only passing glimpses of him; he wears his hair in a bag at the back of his head with what Julia calls ex-bangs falling at all lengths about his face and behind his ears, he is small and slender and I never see him that for the first second I do not think it is a woman, the manner of his dress and his apron add to the delusion. He is never seen with anything on his head in the shape of head gear, and the steward never steps outside of the door without some sort of covering, a cap usually, in windy weather secured by means of a hamper cord tied gracefully beneath the chin. In very hot weather he sports a soft felt hat that would put to blush anything ever worn by Buffalo Bill or any of his class. What his idea is in wearing such a hot, heavy head covering in boiling weather we have never been able to determine. He is the only fat Chinaman we have ever seen but we do not wonder that he is stout for he is a most enormous eater and frighfully lazy and so slow and stupid that it takes him days to grasp the simple suggestion, and he would not take a gait faster than the slow saunter that he assumes on his numerous trips to the galley if we were all in convulsions and our lives depended upon the hot water he was sent to bring. He is a most cowardly fellow, allowing Axel to bully him shamefully, and so improvident and possesses as little judgement that we should probably be without stores before the trip were half over if the Captain, seeing how matters were working, had not taken matters into his own hands and doled the stores out to him in very small quantities.

Axel is a sturdy little Norseman, hardly speaking intelligible English when he joined us at Philadelphia; he now prides himself upon his proficiency in that language. He is very sweet-tempered and helpful, seeming to be only too delighted to wait upon us, and making queer little bows or curtseys when presented with any article of wearing apparel or choice bits from our stores. Axel is only seventeen and has all a boy's love for mischief and fun, as we find occasionally when he overcomes his natural shyness and a little feeling of awe that I think he feels for the feminine portion of the household; on each occasion he suddenly discovers rats running about some portion of the deck near us, or when he slyly sprinkles Julia with salt water as she is lying asleep in her hammock. Axel's special care is the baby and very devoted to him he is too and oftentimes varies the baby's somewhat monotonous diet with some Norse preparation that proves both appetizing and nourishing. The baby repays him by giving him his most devoted love; indeed Axel's delight being un-

14

bounded when the baby absolutely refuses to leave no matter what inducement is offered by members of the family. But after three weeks of sucking, poulticing and salving a finger threatened with a felon, Axel magnaminously announced that the baby loved "Mees" Gould almost as well as he did him and ever after was more devoted than ever in his attentions. If for no other reason I should have been fond of him for his devotion to the unfortunate cats which were an unending misery to me, for they took more unkindly to the life on board ship and from the time we left Philadelphia until we reached the Falklands they were not off my mind. No one cared for them if Axel were not about. I had to seize upon any stray man, not an officer, to feed them for they were kept in what was called the lazaretto (a portion of the "between decks," partitioned off for the stores) which could only be reached by a leap of four feet or so into the depths.

Eternal warfare was waged between Axel and the steward, the cause being the attempt on the part of the steward to make Axel "sir" him; the Captain was often called in to settle the dispute. It is needless to say Axel never gave in; my sympathies were always with him and as the Captain backed the steward we might have had quite stirring times, if we had not felt obligated to slip in and separate the belligerent pair.

The first mate was a mild, inoffensive little man from Calais, Maine but another such a gossip I never knew; if an attack of rheumatic fever had not driven him to a hospital a few weeks after his arrival in San Francisco he would probably be spinning yarns at the present moment, with one of us for his victim. I always withdrew when he appeared on the after-deck in the day watch, for that was his time to narrate his experiences; his former superior officers and their wives suffered then one may be sure.

The second mate, Mr. Dow, a very unworthy member of the Portland family by that name, was much more desirable to look upon in many respects and was much more agreeable than his next superior officer. He had evidently occupied a very different position in life, being very well educated and has the most impressive manners; his firm, well developed athletic figure not as yet being much affected by that cause of all his woes--drink. He however assigned quite a different reason for his troubles. One lovely moonlight night Mrs. Whitmore and I were alone on deck and Mr. Dow (whose watch it was) hovered about us, in a very unusual way for him, and finally burst out in a most confidential strain. He informed us that he had a wife and two children in Boston whom he loved devotedly and for whom he had always provided a most comfortable house, until on an unfortunate day his father-in-law died and his mother-in-law came to make her home with them then--no more happiness in that quiet house, no more delight in his children, no more pride in his wife and then it was, in his unhappiness, that he was driven and drink had driven him this--this a second mate on a merchant ship on a four months voyage. He had a fine command of language and was really quite eloquent, we were so surprised and touched that this very quiet and taciturn man should so open his heart to us, that carried away by his own eloquence he might have gone on for hours, we sitting there, if the man at the wheel, not at all moved by this harrowing tale, had not struck six bells and Mrs. Whitmore suddenly bethought herself that it was time for us to be in bed.

After being a month or two at sea news becomes such a rare and valuable article that the smallest bit is seized upon and with the greatest avidity. Imagine then our joy, our rapture, our eagerness to impart this large and exciting stock of the desired article to the other members of the family. Grave doubts as to the manner of receiving it if wakened at that time of the night led us to refrain for the time being, but the next morning at breakfast we told the whole story, expecting the others to be quite overcome.

To do Julia justice, I think she was much impressed with the fact that the very mysterious Mr. Dow had actually disclosed the secrets of his life and heart. As for the Captain, he only scoffed at the idea and hinted that he was willing to wager a good deal that Boston was not the only city that harbored a devoted Mrs. Dow and delighted, no doubt, they all were to be well rid of him, for another such a growler he never had aboard ship.

Of the crew and our unhappy experience with the mutinies portion I speak at length further on. We have sixteen men designated "able bodied seamen" of almost as many nationalities. The first night on board they are all mustered on deck, placed in a long line and the mate and second mate station themselves before them. The first mate selects a man, the one he considers the most desirable of the lot, then the second mate makes his choice and so on, choosing alternately until the sixteen are chosen. The men of the first mate's watch are then ordered to the fo'castle on the port side, and the other watch to the starboard side, and there they remain. I rarely saw a man away from his side of the ship unless when at work and they were scattered all about. The day

16

(a day at sea is from noon to noon) is divided into six watches of four hours each, except the afternoon watch from four to eight, that being divided into two, that from six to eight being the day watch, the play time of the men off duty. The watches are kept alternately by the men of the starboard and port watches. The watches alternate each day, as the men who are on deck from eight to twelve p.m. tonight, tomorrow might well have only one watch, that from one to four a.m. The bells are struck every half hour, the even numbers on the hour, the odd on the half, eight, twelve, and four being eight bells. The clock in the binnacle regulates all other clocks and watches on the ship as the bells are struck by this. The binnacle clock is set each day at noon when the Captain takes the sight.

The work begins with washing down decks at four a.m. and ends at six p.m. with coiling ropes. That is when it is moderately light and warm. In cold weather, as at the Cape, no work is done on deck that is not absolutely necessary for the well-being of all concerned; at such times the men spend their working hours in the sail room, working or preparing to work on the sails needing repairs.

When working about the deck in the after part of the ship the men are very quiet but let them begin at the ropes, especially when both watches are called out, then it is bedlam let loose. They can't pull at the smallest rope (I should not say "rope" for they say there is only one on board ship and that is the one fastened to the bucket which is used to draw up sea-water for the purpose of testing the temperature) without giving utterance to the most blood-curdling yells. One man called the "shantee" man, we called him the "champion howler," howls for the half day. We rarely understand what our howler says when he is pulling at a brace or line. A brawny Irishman always began with a "Now bend your backs boys, O-ho-ho," and a Peruvian with the most languishing black eyes and of the utmost good nature, unless he is exasperated beyond endurance, has a song in his own language of a very sad character we decided, for it always terminates in a long drawn out and heart rending wail. The more he pulls the more excited he becomes and the louder he wails, until one night it haunted my dreams and Mrs. Whitmore thought I had gone quite mad when I implored her to call the Captain for the Peruvian was insane from a sun-stroke and was about to attack the whole ship's company. I was finally persuaded to wake up and be assured that the man was safe and was neither sun or moon struck. Of one thing I am certain, if I were in the exact center of the North American continent, as far as I could

17

be from the sea, one wail of that voice would bring on a dangerous attack of sea-sickness.

Many times during the first three weeks at sea I attributed sudden attacks of nausea to the frantic howlings of that wretched crew, sometimes there would be three or four sets of them in different parts of the ship and one in each lot howling like a demon, each man going it in a different key and in a different language.

In hoisting sail one man sings a line or two, the others as they pull join in the chorus. This is usually a more pleasing and agreeable sound to us for sail is only set after a gale and glad enough are we when the voices assured us that the wind was subsiding and we may expect clear seas.

February 27

A doldrum and where one is not to be expected too; we seem to strike the unexpected everywhere. We are supposed to have left the S.E. trades behind us but hoped to strike something in the shape of a breeze at once, but not so. The morning was enlivened by several cries of "shark, shark," and calls for shark-hook and fork, I was on deck when the fish was first discovered so was on hand to watch his movements, he proved to be a very small specimen, swimming near the surface of the water he seemed about the size of a large catfish. The hook was duly baited and thrown over and after a little he smelt or sighted the tempting morsel and came playing about the stern, but although I dangled the bait about very alluringly he declined to partake, and as the sun was pouring down upon us, we fastened the line to the rail and withdrew to the shade of the awning.

The water all about us has, all day, been covered with what is called "whale's food," which looks like a fine scum and has a fishy smell. The minute particles which make up this scum are a low form of animal and when seen in the evening have a phosphorescent glow but before evening a breeze had sprung up and we saw nothing of it. We saw no whales during the day. The Captain thinks the water much too warm for them, the temperature of the water at noon being 81 degrees and air 84 degrees. During the greater part of the day there has been no breeze and the sun shining directly upon the water and the white woodwork of the ship has made the day a particularly trying one to unfortunates with weak eyes. The heat does not trouble me as it does some members of the family, nothing like some of our hot August days at home.

There has been quite a little swell and as often as the ship sank into the depths of a long swell, the sails would swing about and we would enjoy quite a little breeze.

I spent the morning in the after part of the wheel-house (my special retreat, on rainy days as well as pleasant, the only difficulty being the ropes and the long bar that constitutes the rudder taking so much room and being too important to be crowded, makes the remaining space rather cramped for us both, but very comfortable for one) there being doors opposite I am sure to get all the air possible and I find the light much less trying than that outside. Reclining on my rug on the floor I read one of Dr. McE.'s sermons to Julia and the Captain sitting under the awning outside, also a few chapters of *Ben Hur* to the Captain.

Later we opened our box of books and distributed a few choice selections among the men. It is quite funny to watch them. We usually place those that we think will interest them in a chair outside, Julia sits in the doorway with paper and pencil to take the names and I sit inside at the open box and make suggestions. Contrary to our expectations they seize upon Clark Russell's productions with eagerness. One man remarked, when we spoke of one as being a "sea" story, that he would take something else for, for his part he was tired of the sea. Another man said he would have a story, for he did not like novels. Another, Murphy by name, a man who has already given the Captain much trouble, selected Irving's *Astoria.*

Speaking of Clark Russell's yarns, we gave *A Strange Voyage* to Mr. Goodwin, the first mate, to read, and for some nights he came aft to report progress to us and every night he seemed more astonished, he said he had "followed" the sea for eighteen years and he had never been through half what those people experienced in three weeks.

In the afternoon we saw a steamer in the distance, and nearer, but some little distance from the ship, an immense turtle but not the eatable kind the Captain said. We also saw a small fish, the like of which had never been seen before. It was not more than six inches long and had what appeared to be two sets of wings or else its tail had fan-like projections on either side, its color was a beautiful light green and it swam or flew just below the surface of the water. The day closed with a beautiful sunset, not so wonderful as the one a few nights earlier when the moon was smaller.

The evening closed with the excitement of a report of light on our starboard bow. The Captain had gone below but appeared at once and decided it was that of a steamer bound north, she passed very near us and if it had only been daylight we could have signaled her.

I forgot to say the men caught the shark and we had a good look at it. It was evidently very young, the carpenter assured us that sharks of that age "was good eating." It was fried for their supper.

Monday, February 28

The Captain announced that the sharp shower of Saturday night had given us plenty of rain water and we could scrub to our hearts' content. As water is an object on a long voyage every drop is utilized, consequently we took turns at it, and as I led the procession to the tubs I had decidedly the best of it, for Mrs. Whitmore announced at dinner that she did her washing in my rinse water, it is needless to say she brought up the rear. With Axel to hang out, and take in and run to the galley for hot irons, four p.m. saw our washing and ironing finished to the last piece. The sun in those latitudes is a very good helper in the laundry line, several pieces of a very grayish tint, when hung out, came in white and unspotted.

After being so very industrious in this direction Julia and I decided to loaf, so we finished the day with reading aloud and playing, as a set out, four games of cribbage, the winner at the close of the voyage to be feasted by the loser. As I am just learning the game it is not difficult to prophesy as to the probable hostess on that occasion. A brisk breeze all day which wafted us one hundred and eighty miles on our way, a lovely sunset, a moon light evening and gymnastics on the house just before going to bed finish the day.

Tuesday, March 1

Dead calm most of the day, damp, hot and disagreeable generally. A sharp shower in the night killed the wind but did not effect the sea much. Sole excitement the sight of a distant vessel, pronounced by the Captain to be a hermaphrodite brig bound for Montevideo. Lovely vessel. Later a shower which drove us to the forward cabin and games of cribbage, said games placing Julia five nearer being entertained in San Francisco.

Saturday, March 5

This has been a most disagreeable week, a heavy sea running and no wind to speak of, and what little we have had being a contrary direction. The glass is running very low and the Captain thinks there must have been a heavy gale near us, but we only came in for its effects upon the sea.

Julia had a touch of sea-sickness on Wednesday. I felt much pleased that I had no qualms, but as I had to sit with folded hands all day, when not asleep, owing to severe pain in my eyes I do not know that I gained much.

On Friday we attempted to signal a passing bark, but as she was slow in running up her signals we only know that she was Norwegian, and hope she understood our signals and will report us "all well," if she should be bound to a Swedish port. I am afraid the friends at home will not have their anxieties much lessened by our attempt.

This morning the first I heard was "sail ho!" and "The Captain thinks we can send letters home." As there was a dead calm and not so very much sea, it seemed possible that we might board her with mail. I dressed hurriedly and rushed on deck, the vessel was some distance off, but making for us. After breakfast we anxiously watched and I even began a letter but the date and "Dear Mother" made me so homesick that I concluded to wait a little. Very soon Captain Whitmore broke it to us gently that she was a French bark bound for Havre. I am much afraid that the non-arrival of letters will cause much anxiety at home, for the Captain spoke so positively of being able to send letters by returning ships. We have had [one word] enough I am sure but returning ships are wanting, we have seen so few and never where we expected to meet dozens.

This week has been distinguishable in two ways. During it we have glided tranquilly from the tropic to the temperate zone, a change much noticed from a decided lowering of the temperature, especially during the afternoons and from the lengthening of the the twilight, the last Julia and I much enjoy as it gives us an extra game or two. The first change necessitates an alteration in the manner of our dress, light underwear and muslin gowns are things of the past and we now appear in ginghams and satins in the morning and woolens in the afternoon. At this point it is well to notice the important part my beautiful blue muslin gown has played upon this voyage. I will mention for the enlightenment of the ignorant that on the day before I left home it was resurrected from the depths of an attic packing trunk, where its beauties had long been hidden.

I certainly have found it most comfortable during the heat of the last two weeks. I am afraid I shall find nothing in my wardrobe as comfortable for the hot weather on the other side, if we are so happy as to round the Cape safely.

Now I am on the subject I will say that if the event itself (rounding Cape Horn, I mean) even half way equals the preparations and prognostications I can only say "Woe unto us," for the preparations are gigantic and the prophecies dire. So far I have refused to be scared and at the present moment feel that a Cape Horn gale might create a welcome diversion, however I speak as one who knoweth not whereof she speaketh. To speak truly everything that has been done about the ship for the last six weeks, has been done with an eye to this position of our passage, our great annoyance we have borne patiently, owing to constantly received assurances that our safety depended upon its being well done. Consequently when we are awakened at five a.m. by a tremendous not hammering but pounding, seemingly directly under our berths, a pounding that actively raises each separate hair on one's head from the jar, when this goes on day after day our sufferings lessened only as the pounding recedes a little from our part of the ship, one may be sure that it is a pretty powerful reason that makes us endure it with any grace whatever, especially Mrs. Whitmore as the baby catches only the shortest of naps and is naturally very troublesome.

All this means that the seams in the hold are being stuffed with oakum and then hot pitch poured on to make them water tight; caulked I believe it is called and I think the carpenter must fully appreciate the word. For however hot it is on deck it is doubly so in the hold, and as the walls are not more that three and one-half feet high, anything like an upright position is impossible, so no one can wonder that the poor man comes out very red as to his face, much bent as to his knees and back (his neck having been already broken, according to his story. We can detect no extra bend in that.) and a strong odor of pitch hanging about him. However his woes are somewhat mitigated and his courage kept up by a daily call from the Captain "to come down and set the clock," the clock still needs attention but since that particular job is over the carpenter is no longer called in, for the last two days I am happy to say we have lived in peace.

The cargo has been overlooked as, notwithstanding Mr. Davis' boast in Philadelphia that we should have no trouble with our cargo (Mr. Davis being the stevedore) some of the iron water-pipes shifted a little when we first came out from Philadelphia and rolled about us in quite a lively manner, in fact some of the pipes were injured; new sails have been bent to the yards, old ropes, only they are not called ropes but clew-lines and buntlines, are changed for new and even the steward designates different stores as "nuff to last and no last round Cape Horn." So all things are being prepared, even our minds for the dreaded and supreme moment, several moments I am afraid, for "rounding Cape Horn" means passing from fifty degrees S. latitude on this side to fifty degrees S. on the other. However if this state of things continues we are liable to spend the rest of the four months, allowed for our trip, in getting to the Cape.

The other event, spoken of as distinguishing this week, has been the departure, no more to return, of potatoes from our bill of fare. This is really a great loss to me, for whatever else I have I always want potatoes. I thought it would be as when the other vegetables and apples gave out, I did not miss them at all as I thought I should, but I find potatoes as almost the "sine qua non" and the "dandy" something or other "funk" (I believe) which appeared simultaneously with their departure not at all a substitute. This "dandy-funk" is hard bread chopped or pounded and made into a kind of a hash, without meal, but held together with butter and water; the sailors had the honor of naming it I believe. I will say now that I shall not mourn the departure of onions as I have potatoes, and when they see fit to glide from the scene I shall bear the loss with great composure, for onions have been almost the bane of my existance on this trip, I hate them always and to have them served, raw or cooked, three times a day and have any member of the family except myself, partake thereof, is a little more that I can bear, then too I think I have never quite recovered from the effect of the scent of them when I was sea-sick, and am not sure I ever shall.

Sunday, March 6

No sun, some rain, much damp, light sea, moderate wind, nothing to say.

Monday, March 7

As we are approaching the mouth of the river Plate and as things look rather threatening, the Captain thinks best to make all fast, for gales are prevalent in this quarter at all seasons of the year. Consequently, much to our regret, our awning was taken down this morning, and packed away and we were requested to look over our box of books and take out enough to last round the Cape. The box with its cover on hinges and padlocked has hitherto occupied a prominent position in the after wheel-house, it is now consigned to the depths of the hold where there will be no danger of its getting a wetting unless the after part of the ship be carried away.

This same after wheel-house is such a refuge to me that I think it deserves special mention. The wheel-house, as its name implies, is devoted to the steering apparatus of the ship, the after wheel-house is that part of the house not devoted to the compass, the wheel and the man; it is separated by a single board partition from the forward part, and is much the larger portion. Its advantages are many, it has doors opposite by which means a breath of air is possible, even on the hottest day, and a roof as protection from light and heat. Add to these the long book box placed near the door sheltered by the awning and offering, with the aid of rugs and pillows, a most inviting lolling place. With a lovely outlook on sea and sky and you have the most delightful retreat possible.

To this haven I fled when partly recovered from sea-sickness, my weak head and weaker eyes making the heat of the cabin and the bright sun or the rain of the deck alike intolerable.

Now in preparation for gales the box is removed and two chairs are lashed side by side in its place and a very elegant portiere, of canvas, tacked to the door as a protection from the wind.

Here we expect to spend hours when it is not cold or wet or windy on deck and we tire of the cabin, here we keep our cribbage board, rugs and the place is spoken of as our "boudoir." Alas! that there should be disadvantages in such an Eden, but even so. Our greatest trial is the after-bell which hangs almost over our heads and is struck with varying emphasis, according to the disposition of the man presiding at the wheel, every half hour; one would suppose we would grow accustomed to the sound and regularity of its striking but no, each time our ears are deafened and our souls harrowed within us by the suddeness of the shock. A lesser evil are the ropes, pulleys and bars of wood meandering about the room, which makes it difficult for any but the experienced to steer one's way safely. The Captain fears that we shall get wounded or bung up, ours that we shall impede the navigation of the ship.

Tuesday, March 8

The preparations being all made for a gale, naturally no gale came. Today the sun is shining and a fresh breeze blowing and the color of the water announced to the uninitiated that we were nearer shore, or "on soundings" and that the waters of the river Plate was giving a lighter tinge to the color of the deep; for two or three days, the Captain says, the water will be this beautiful aquamarine tint, while we are crossing the "mouth" of this great river. The weather is much colder, additional clothing is necessary and woolen gowns the order of the day.

Tomorrow, Wednesday, is to be the great day, "the day we celebrate" as the first officer expresses it, which means it is the ninth of March and my birthday, but as the whole family, including Captain and Mrs. Whitmore, and the baby, the first mate, Julia and myself are to have birthdays this trip, birthdays, to say the least, will not be a novelty. However, mine leads the van, a slight distinction in my favor.

Wednesday, March 9

Seemed to be a day made specially to order for in place of the expected gale or high cold winds and rough sea, there was a beautiful blue sky, perfectly cloudless, a sea blue as the sky, and a gentle breeze and at eight a.m. so warm that the Captain ordered the awning spread. So when I came on deck at 8:30 I found the family seated comfortably about under the awning waiting to offer congratulations, and surely never before upon any birthday of mine was I greeted with air and sky so balmy and June-like or was I ever arrayed in garb so summery.

Baby with his moving and congratulatory kiss presented me with a beautiful plush opera-glass case, in the choice of which his mama probably had much more of a hand than he; however I was much pleased as I also was with a handkerchief I had carefully helped Julia to select while shopping in Philadelphia. Besides the handkerchief I found upon the breakfast table a little note of congratulations from the Captain and Mrs. Whitmore with the verse for the day. Mr. Goodwin presented me with a peg in place of one missing from the cupboard. Later I opened a little package given me by Emily Thacher just before leaving home and found a cute little satin bag containing boot buttons, linen thread, and needles, a very satisfactory and handy gift in this shopless

25

waste.   The plans for the celebration of the day had been many and varied, but as all centered about the grand birthday cake, brought with such care from home, it was first brought out and duly admired.

The purity of its outward aspect was somewhat impaired by exposure to moisture and heat, but the inside was in no wise effected and was pronounced a great success by the united family.   It was speedily reduced to slices, sixteen of which were wrapped in white paper and tied with colored string a la wedding cake.   The mate, who had already viewed the magnificent whole and had retired, as it was his watch below, was sent a slice, each member of the family was presented with a portion, the baby receiving a very small piece of the frosting, and then the carpenter was sent for.   As the carpenter has a slight drawl and is rather spicy in his observations we anticipated much amusement from his remarks.   A very small glass was filled with some of the Captain's choice whiskey, as we were afraid he might not otherwise appreciate the cake, and we sat down arrayed in our best garments to wait his arrival.   He came but he said he was sick, and he did look badly, however he rallied at the sight of the whiskey, drank my health with much heartiness, wished me happiness and a hundred birthdays, which last considering the number already passed, was not a wish that I could very heartily second.

The second mate, Mr. Dow, was next sent for; he received the cake and the libation with stateliness, congratulated me with great dignity and went off bearing his cake with him.   Mr. Dow was requested to send in the men of his watch one by one.   The first to arrive was an American, so he not knowing what to expect, marched in bravely enough and through the ordeal very creditably to himself, drank his whiskey, made his bow, offered his congratulations and withdrew bearing his cake with him.   I have no doubt the others after learning what was before them, although by no means despising the refreshment, would have preferred weathering the fiercest of Cape Horn gales to coming to the cabin under such circumstances.   The German element as a rule were most at their ease and most liberal with their good wishes; one in particular, whom we called "Mrs. Whitmore's favorite," was very gentlemanly in his demeanor, from his peculiar dress, which is very neat as well as nautical. The Captain judges it quite possible that he may have been a deserter from the German navy. Most of the men proffered their "respects" and one wished me a "Merry Christmas" and all were rather shaky as to their hands and knees.   However they all seemed pleased with the attention, but whether they would be willing to repeat the performance

26

for the sake of the plunder, I can't say. I forgot to mention the very pleasing attention offered me by the Captain, that of flying all the flags, ensigns and signals on the ship, as the signal flags are of many and very brilliant colors it was a very pretty sight, the only regret was that there were no other ships about to see our finery, but the Captain said if one should see us we should have all hands aboard us at once, as they would think everything was the matter, with the whole code flying at once.

With a run on the house in the afternoon with Julia and a lovely moonlight evening on deck I finished the day. A day very happily spent, thanks to the efforts of all the friends and which without this kindness might have been very forlorn and one not easy to get through with.

Murphy, one of the men and generally considered a ring-leader where there is any trouble with the crew, distinguished himself when he came for his cake. He is a tall, well-built, rather good-looking man, an American born Irishman, but speaks without a brogue, not easily intimidated and very "toughy." He drank his whiskey, with his cake and with the lowest kind of a bow said, "The kindest wish I can wish you, Miss Gould, is that you may never have to pass another birthday on board the *Berlin*. The Captain said, "That will do Murphy, leave the cabin," and he left.

Thursday, March 10

Cold, brisk breeze and quite a sea, distinguished in giving us the first sight we had of the bird of much renown, the albatross, and the fish of only less renown, the porpoise. A school of the latter playing about the ship for a short time during the forenoon. These quite came up to my expectations but the albatross I must say I consider a failure. As for the superstition in regard to it I should dare kill a dozen of them and have no more feeling than if they were so many ducks.

The sun set in a cloud and from various indications the officers evidently expect the long delayed gale. As it was disagreeable on deck, we came down early and soon after what there was of the gale was upon us, but the predictions were so much worse than the reality that we hardly noticed it. I, in fact, slept through the most of it; the Captain was anxious however and spent the most of the night on deck.

Friday, March 11

The Captain has braced us all day with a promise of sighting land, so anxious was I of becoming a second and feminine Columbus that I kept a sharp lookout all the morning only to be rewarded by being fast asleep when finally it was sighted in the afternoon. The land seen is that part of the continent just south of the Plate and is described as being a high cliff-like bank, but at our distance, sixteen miles or so, we could discover nothing but sand hills, but it was land and with the glasses we could distinguish the green portion from the red sand or earth, and were happy. I never realized before what a blessed sight it was, as I also never realized before how much of its grandeur the ocean loses when seen in its boundless state. Either the mind is not capable of grasping the illimitable or ungovernable part of it, or the sameness or the dreariness of such a waste of waters strikes to one's heart, there is to me none of the fascination, the almost witchery of the sea-shore ocean, to which I am accustomed.

We sighted land at about four p.m., it kept opening up until seven, when we gradually left it behind us. We have wonderful sunsets nearly every evening, but tonight, with the land to disappear behind, the sun seemed to take his departure with much more grandeur and certainly with more gorgeous coloring than usual. It is utterly impossible for me, with tongue or pen, to do justice to these evening skys, the pinks, the blues and the grays are so gorgeous and the greens and dark blues of such odd and various tints, that the ordinary observer can only enjoy and make no attempt at description (see, however, Julia M. Folsom's log for descriptions of those lovely sunsets).

We had another lovely moonlight night. These are the nights, the moonlight evenings in the South Atlantic that will haunt our dreams for the rest of our natural lives.

March 12

Baby's birthday and because it is his first his parents appear to think it is not necessary to celebrate, the more reason to as it is rather more of a rarity to him than to me, say. The carpenter anxiously inquired if this was to be a celebration, having an eye, no doubt on the liquid portion of the entertainment. There seems to be no more fitting time to sing the baby's charms than on his birthday and such a little dear as he is certainly should have everything lovely said of him.

He does not look like the same child who came out of Philadelphia with us. Salt, fresh air and imperial [one word] have done their best and we have a fat, solid, ruddy little fellow as full of fun, laughter, and cunning little tricks as any one could desire. He has two teeth very apparent to even a casual observer and two more visible, so far, only to the fond eyes of affection, his mother being the only one this far able to discover the new comers.

Axel is very fond of him and is ambitious of teaching him Swedish and as his teaching runs contrary to ours, which consists in excercising him in the art of throwing kisses, moving his hands and such graceful accomplishments and as Axel is with him more than we, the Swedish rather prevails over the hand shakings and kisses.

Within the last two or three days he has learned to creep and such a one-sided, crab-like motion as it is, but he manages to get over the ground or floor astonishingly, he has worn one shoe quite through, as it is not always easy for us to get downtown, his mother looked rather aghast when she discovered the fact.

Such a tousler as he is, a real boy, the more he is shaken and tossed about and the harder the frolic the more he seems to enjoy it. Altogether he is the delight of our eyes and the joy of our hearts and we all agree with his mother when she declares him to be the "sweetest baby on board the ship."

Tonight I distinguished myself by climbing, under the Captain's care and direction, to the mizzen-mast-head, quite a feat in my eyes, as it is something Mrs. Whitmore has never done. One gets a wonderful outlook from such a height and realizes better than ever before the distance from the deck. I appreciate now and heartily respect the nerve possessed by the sailors who go up so much higher and skip about on the ropes and yards with the wind blowing a gale and the ship lurching heavily.

Lovely moonlight nights, but the moon, in these latitudes, has a strange look, to which I cannot become accustomed, the old man reposes peacefully on his side instead of sitting up "peart"-like as he does at home.

Sunday, March 13

Fair breeze all the morning, falling off to our usual calm in the afternoon. Had partial service in the cabin after breakfast and one of P. Brooks' sermons in the wheel-house later on. Mrs. Whitmore's unusual devoutness we attribute to our

29

neighborhood to Cape Horn; said devoutness takes the form of hiding her novel in the wardrobe that it may not tempt her to break the Sabbath.

Tiny land birds have been flying about the ship all day, little brown waifs of the sparrow variety, I think, blown from the land apparently and glad even of a resting place as unstable as our decks and ropes. We had one in the cabin for awhile, offered it bread crumbs and water, it declined the first but seemed glad of the water, at the approach of the baby it flew from my hand to my room where I left it to rest, thinking it sleepy, but I never saw it again, I suppose after resting it attempted to make the land again. The next morning only one was left on the ship and that one expiring in my chair soon after we came on deck. We had a first class funeral which reminded me of my youthful days, only then we used to resurrect the corpse every day or two that we might watch the process of decay. We wrapped the little thing in white cloth, tied it up with white thread and consigned it to its watery grave.

Lovely sunset, lovely evening, moon blood red, rising just before nine looked like a mass of molten metal and so near that seemingly one had only to stretch out one's hand over the stern and grasp a portion.

March 14

Calms, calms, calms!!
Weather warm and lovely. Julia begins to be superstitious if we have such unheard of experiences all along, what will come to us when we reach the Cape. I am not troubled by any such misgivings, I pretend to consider the place a myth, the horrors of which, as set forth in these tales and yarns the products of a diseased imagination and each narration a fresh Cassandra to whose folksayings I decline to listen. I am only moved to express the wish that we may have wind enough to take us round and not be rocked about in the doldrums from fifty to fifty.

One of the lovliest evenings we have had, so calm, that the "painted ship upon a painted ocean" seems no poet's imagination. The two stringed violin comes out strong on its remnants and the men's voices sound particularly clear and sweet. The choice of "Home Sweet Home" may be a little trying to our feelings but "Nellie Gray" has no harrowing tendencies and that one or two others of an unknown nature we enjoy. The Captain, disgusted with the calm goes below and

30

declares that nothing but a breeze will bring him up. Mr. Goodwin does his best to raise a wind by twisting the sails to all quarters but no one but himself is able to perceive the slightest symptom. Towards ten p.m. two clouds appear, one from the south and one from the north, which promise to bring us a wind and the direction, whether fair or head, depends upon the cloud that prevails. I bet as heavily as my limited means will allow on the cloud from the south and the head wind, Mr. Goodwin against me. Julia and I stayed up as long as we could to watch the struggle, but as the cloud from the north appeared to be gaining and as a few drops of rain came, we gave it up and went below.

March 15

Like the railings of the small boys of Bible fame, our mockings reacted upon ourselves. The black cloud from the south came up and devoured the black cloud from the north and the evils, a high head wind and short, choppy sea are upon us, to the united power of which Julia and I succumbed both being disgustingly sick.

The peculiarity of my sea-sickness is the fondness my stomach seems to possess for gymnastics. I will be feeling perfectly well apparently, perhaps playing cards, when, all at once my stomach turns a complete somersault and the consequence is I vomit.

It is all over in a moment, and if it is just before dinner I sit down and eat heartily and think no more of it until the next exhibition. Julia, on the other hand, feels a little nausea all the time, but does not vomit.

March 17

St. Patrick's Day! and we are celebrating indeed. These three days, Tuesday, Wednesday and Thursday, have been bad, worse and worst. "Gale, strong gale, and heavy gale," that is the way the Captain designates them in his log. The wind skipping about among the west by S. and W., to W. by S. and S.E. by south points of the compass, a heavy sea and we trying to make some power of westing, the ship being under close-reefed top sails.

It is worth a trip to Cape Horn for the sake of the amount of contentment one will hereafter take in "staying put," not only in regard to one's self but also to articles. I laugh to

31

myself, all the time I am dressing, at the attitudes assumed and the bracings and maneuvers necessary for the accomplishment of the simplest purposes.

Mrs. Whitmore came to my room this morning and announced her intention of keeping me in bed for the ship was rolling so, she thought there might be danger of my being thrown down. Julia had not had a comfortable night and was then reposing on Mrs. Whitmore's bed, and was to have her breakfast sent in to her. I decided I had rather get up and see the fun, so then began those aforementioned gymnastics. I think I have left a full length impression of my figure on one wall of my stateroom, for I invariably bring up at that one spot when the ship begins to roll. Then it requires such agility on my part in order to get to a thing or place and back before a heavy roll comes on and such dexterity in catching flying articles, for the slightest thing, left unanchored for one moment, goes skimming about the room, first one side and then the other, always bringing up at the most inaccessible point.

The poor steward's life is a burden to him on these days, he does not say anything but his face is a study. This morning he left the forward cabin to go to the galley for corn meal mush, he had just gone when a heavy sea struck us and the Captain said "that will catch the steward," and sure enough the outside door was thrown open and in tumbled the steward, mopping the water from his face and with the cover of the dish in his hand. The only remark he made was that "he saw carpenter was overboard once." Every time he goes when we are at the table the Captain tells him he is a most wonderful man and to be sure and come back alive, this pleases him and he manages to smile a little.

Mrs. Whitmore sent Axel to the galley to make the baby's breakfast, he came back with trousers rolled up nearly to his knees and bare feet, said the galley was full of water, from the cook we have not heard. The men go about decked out in oil-skins of every imaginable color, light yellow predominating, and the sun shining and the sky as blue as June. It really is great fun to the [person], but it requires as much effort and the expenditure of as much strength to go from one room to another here as to go downtown on a calm day at home.

The doors leading out on the deck all have what is called wash-boards in them, these are boards varying in height from two to three feet and are so placed that they fill the door-way from the threshold up their own height and are there whether the door is closed or not. They serve to keep the sea from breaking directly into the room whenever the door is opened.

Five-thirty p.m. Just came down from deck. Wind subsiding, sea still high. I would not believe three days could make such a change in our calm and peaceful ocean, and there were such waves except in sea-yarns of the Clark Russell order. The men were making sail and at present my highest ambition is to acquire that peculiar bend of body and legs which enables them to walk to windward when the ship is rolling heavily to leeward. It is a great art, the Captain has given us a few instructions. Three sails have been carried away during the gale, two jibs and upper fore-top sail.

March 18

Mrs. Whitmore and the baby wakened me this morning, Mrs. Whitmore to tell me that land was in sight, a fresh breeze blowing and we were making our course. The land disappeared before I had sight of it, but the Patagonian coast is getting to be such an old story, I did not mind. We spent the most of the morning on deck, clear and bright. Sea comparatively quiet, had mittens on for first time, am wearing my blue flannel gown, find my pea-jacket very comfortable these days, reminds us of November days at home.

Afternoon--nearly dead calm, with heavy gales, wind dead ahead and high sea one day and dead calm the next. I began to understand how it is that ships have been six months rounding the Cape, it would not surprise me if we were to spend the next eight off this coast. If we were near enough we should become familiar with every rill, rivulet and brook from the river Plate to the Straits of Magellan.

March 19

The "likes" of this was never known before. Here we are in the latitudes of perpetual winds, and almost a dead calm, however we should be grateful for even the slightest breeze. Real "ladies weather" the mate calls it, and the blame thereof is about equally divided between us and the two black cats. As the two last mentioned animals were pronounced "lucky" at the start, and as a sacrifice is to be made it bids fair to fall upon Julia and myself unless we succeed in drawing attention to the cats. We consulted the carpenter yesterday and Mrs. Whitmore taxed him with advising us to pin our faith to black cats, but he declares it a libel as all he had said was that some particular bone, of a wholly black cat, would bring luck. Consequently if this weather continues the cats will have to go for the sake of the bone, we are not sure as to the bone, but if the whole frame-work is preserved we shall probably strike the right one.

The Captain fumes and frets and nearly works himself sick worrying over the state of affairs, is continually sighting land, studies his chart, consults the patent log and is continually declaring that he never before experienced weather like this in this region. We all ignore the subject, praise the warmth and brightness and try to appear perfectly contented and not to harrow his feelings with any signs of impatience. However he has not yet arrived at the point of tearing out his hair or up his chart, as, Mrs. Whitmore assures us, some captains are moved to do when exasperated beyond endurance.

Sunday, March 20

Today we started to "round Cape Horn," this being the manner of expressing the passing from fifty degrees S. latitude on the Atlantic side to the same degree on the Pacific side. We passed into the stormy latitude in a roaring hurricane, as there was no rain only violent wind coming in gusts and squalls. I stayed out as long as possible, to watch the men taking in sails. All hands were on deck, of course, and it needed sharp work to save the sails, as it was, two were carried away, but they were on the fore-mast and I did not get the full benefit. I clung to the life rail in front of the wheelhouse as long as possible, then retired to the forward wheelhouse and hung out of the window there; the man at the wheel being good natured, assured me I was not in the way. Julia gave it up and went in at an early stage of the proceedings but I stuck it out until all the sails were safe and the gale subsiding somewhat.

When I finally went below I found that I was thoroughly chilled, having been gently sprinkled with salt water once or twice during the excitement of the morning. A hot ginger tea and a warm bath set me up and I took no cold.

March 21

We have had the snow-capped, indeed one might say snow-clad mountains of Tierra del Fuego in sight nearly all day. It has been a lovely sight. The mountains are not in a continous line as the Green Mountains are but are distinct mountains massed together, so as we change our position new peaks are continously coming up and out from behind the foremost ones. The air is as clear and the sky and water as bright a blue as possible and the clear white of the mountains shows beautifully against the intense background of blue sky and across the foreground of blue water.

It is so cold we cannot stay out for long unless we are taking brisk exercise, so we stay only a short time and come out often and each time we are surprised and delighted with some new view. It really seems to me I never saw a lovlier sight. Then I think of my beloved Vienna [Maine] view, or the outlook from the top of our mountain in Vienna and I think I will not say it is the finest I have ever seen. The fact that I have been so long with only the ocean to look out upon no doubt adds to my enjoyment and then I have never before seen mountains so covered with snow.

Tonight our mountains were lighted up or glorified by a most gorgeous sunset. There were none of the delicate sunset tints of the tropics, but the red, flame color and orange, to which we are accustomed at home, shone upon and over, through and around our "delectable mountains," now just disappearing peak by peak from our view, the more distant and shadowed ones being of darker shades of blue, even black in places. So we saw them last and so we shall always remember them.

March 22

The Captain loves to have an excuse for calling us up early. If it were not that Mrs. Whitmore mercifully intervenes in our behalf, I really think he would have the one or other of us on deck hours before breakfast every morning. This morning he had an excellent excuse and he made the most of it. The first thing I heard was "Staten Land in sight, get up and see the lighthouse." I responded promptly for a wonder and was on deck some time before Julia appeared on the scene. Staten Land is such a barren spot and has a look so peculiar to itself that the Captain was very anxious for us to see it. The Chiliean Government has just erected a lighthouse there, the first one that has ever been there and I think the only one so far south, and although the Captain and Mrs. Whitmore had seen the preparations, they had never seen it completed and consequently be light. We saw the land and the light. How a few hundred dollars a year can tempt man, woman or child to live in that bleak spot I cannot see.

We spent considerable time planning the lives of poor unfortunates doomed to live there. I think it could be made a convict station with good effect. Siberia itself could not be worse for north of this land is Tierra del Fuego with its miles and miles of mountains never free from snow and south is Cape Horn and land, which from all I hear, for barreness and inaccessibility, would put to blush any Siberian waste as portrayed by the most gifted novelist.

The land itself is one vast rock where nothing grows and which offers a home to sea-birds only, thousands of which were circling about us. The island seemed to be as near to us as Squirrel Island to Southport [Maine], but was really much farther away and looked as Monhegan [Maine] does, to one approaching it from the Boothbay [Maine] or western side. Indeed there was much to remind me of my beloved Monhegan, although the latter is not so barren and its eastern side is much more precipitous, but Staten Land, when we saw it was covered with a bright green moss, which looked like vegetation and the lighthouse gave it a slight appearance of being inhabited.

The light, instead of being located upon the highest point of land (or rock rather) is snuggled down in a little cave-like place, much more cozy and desirable for the inhabitants probably than a more exposed position, but hardly as effective for mariners.

Fortified by a pocketful of sweet-crackers and "a little something hot," we stayed out until breakfast time and we had rounded the eastern and opened up the southern and western portions of the land, each more desolate than that which went before.

Desolate seems to be the proper term to apply to the land in this portion of the globe, for it is the personification of desolation. There are no trees, large or small, not even of the scrub pine or fir variety which we see growing in the most exposed places north; on most of the islands there is no moss, only cold, bare, gray rocks, not a cheering prospect certainly on a cold, windy, stormy winter's day. We saw Staten Land under the most favorable circumstances and the moss which covered every portion and filled every crack and cranny of the rock quite cheered us with its greeness.

As for the savages, cannibal, "the lowest order of mankind," who are said to occupy these wastes, I take no stock whatever in them. No dog could survive for a month on one of these islands, let alone a man even if he were a cannibal and the "lowest order," etc. Still, Captain Whitmore tells us of seeing men and women standing to their necks in water in the Straits of Magellan in mid-winter with the cliffs on either side of the Straits covered with snow and ice, banks so precipitous and ice so thick that the steamers had only to back up to the bank and cut out all the ice needed for the refrigerators. Constitutions and spirits that could stand that amount of cold and wet might possible look upon Staten Land and its neighboring islands as sort of paradise. There would, at least, be solid foundation beneath them and the mists and fog hanging about, are not quite as thick as water.

March 23

Bright, lovely weather, cold as our November weather in Maine but just right for brisk runs on the deck. Captain Whitmore is very anxious about the winds, he hoped that the new moon today would bring us an east wind, which if we were in a position, would waft us round the Cape in fine style. Consequently he has taken advantage of every zephyr and we are far enough south to clear the Cape, but the east wind cometh not and the Captain has gloomy predictions in regard to some innocent looking clouds in the northwest. Our present breeze is dying out, at any rate, and unless we have a doldrum, as I have prophecied all along, we must have a wind from some quarter.

Sighted a small vessel, either a brig or barkentine, another unfortunate bound round the Cape, too far away to signal.

We began now to hear what has never been whispered in our presence before, that March, with her equinoctial gales, is the worst possible month, with the exception of October, in which to pass the Cape. Surely the reality can't surpass the predictions. We can't be more than three months getting round that and six days being the two extremes on record.

March 24 and 25

Two more days of rolling and tumbling, two more days of mad playing, of desperate clutchings, of wild graspings and attempts of reaching after the unattainable, the unattainable being in this case a stationary object or a place of rest.

If violent exercise will make muscles, ours will be of iron and if this condition of affairs continues much longer, the more vulnerable portions of our bodies will be the color of the above mentioned metal, perhaps copper, of a greenish hue, would be a better comparison.

We pass the greater part of these days in our berths, as we are better able to brace ourselves in a small space; with pillows at our backs and blankets tucked about us, one at the foot and the other at the head of the berth, sardine fashion, Julia and I manage to pass the time very comfortably. We take turns reading aloud, at present we are devoting ourselves to the *Fair God* and Bancroft's *History of the U. S.* with a few of the *Peppermint Perkin's Letters* thrown in to leaven the rest. We are very careful to read only two or three of these at a time and usually just before going to bed, that we may finish off the day with a good laugh.

I have reason to thank Emily Thacher many times during this trip, for her thoughtful efforts to add to my comfort, but as she bestowed of the P. P.'s letters she almost outdid herself. We look upon these as a very precious possession for no matter how forlorn and knocked about we feel, a letter from Peppermint brightens us at once.

Now that there is so much water flying about, the shutters and double shutters have to be closed on the weather side and even on the skylights, for salt water backed by a strong wind has a wonderful penetrating power, even protected in this way small rivulets are seen running down from the windows and meandering about the floor. Consequently one great disadvantage of the rough weather is the dark state rooms, fortunately Julia's and my rooms are on opposite sides of the ship, so one or the other is light, and to that one we retire and proceed to make ourselves comfortable as I have described.

Another great disadvantage is the helter-skelter manner with which our meals are necessarily served. Our soup comes on in bowls, our tea in immense mugs, until I rebelled against the mugs, I preferred to spill my tea to burying my entire face in a thick, white, ware mug. Mrs. Whitmore has had the worst luck of all. One morning the syrup pitcher took a header in her direction and emptied nearly the whole of its contents in her lap; next the pickle bottle took a turn to leeward and with vinegar flying brought up in her plate. Her last adventure was with the hot water pitcher. I saw the last mentioned article going and made a clutch at it, but away it went and hot water was freely sprinkled over Mrs. Whitmore's arm and wrist; this last accident she bore with much better grace than either of the others, although as the water was hot, we were prepared for an outcry.

If one puts down one's knife or fork for an instant, the next they may be on the floor or on the other side of the table. Truly to keep one's seat at the table, a cup or glass in an upright, a plate in a horizontal position and to use one's knife and fork at the same time--to say nothing of frantic efforts in behalf of bread-plates and vegetable dishes in the center of the table, to do all this requires no mean amount of dexterity and skill.

The table has racks all about it and railings around the edge so that one has to assume a particularily graceful, sloping position, with elbows out-spread, in order to reach over these barriers. The water pitcher and the most necessary articles from the caster have separate racks, which fit into the middle space into which the table is divided.

We have dominoes at this table, some of these rough afternoons, the Captain being very fond of the game, and as nuts and raisins seem to be a proper accompaniment, if we feel remarkably agile we partake, but I must say the played and unplayed dominoes, nuts, shells, raisins, dishes, and nutcrackers get decidedly mixed sometimes, and when the baby comes to join the fray confusion reigns.

One thing adds much to our discomfort during these gales. Whenever the wind is at all strong, there is a very suspicious rolling and rumbling below, and during the last two days, the disturbance has been much increased. I knew that we started our cargo when we first came out from Philadelphia, for in the fine weather of the tropics the Captain had some of it restowed and he hoped these would be no further trouble, but it seems that his hopes are in vain. A considerable portion of our cargo is made up of iron, either raw material or made into definite articles. The large iron water-pipes (used in cities for carrying water about) is the part that is giving us trouble. There are two or three sizes and all heavy and unwieldy, very liable to give trouble; these pipes have started now and are rolling about the hold from side to side and as the ship lurches and rolls about new pipes are started and tier after tier is undermined; just how badly off we are or whether anything can be done, can only be decided when the sea calms down enough to allow the hatches to be opened and the men to go down and investigate.

After my usual custom I have been able to sleep all night, no matter how rough or stormy it might be, but last night the noise in the hold was too much for me. I had to acknowledge this morning that I had lost several hours sleep and the Captain said more, in regard to the trouble, than I have ever heard him say before. He owns that he has been and is still very anxious, but he can't judge of the danger until he can go below, always before he has spoken of it in a very matter-of-fact way.

Tonight the wind is going down, but there is a very heavy gale.

March 26

A very disagreeable night, none of us sleeping much, I imagine. It seemed to me that I passed the night trying to make myself as light as possible, after the fashion people have of trying to lighten their weight in going over dangerous places. As the ship lurched and rolled to one side, it seemed as if a mountain of moveable matter beneath us started and rolled to leeward, with a noise of very heavy, distant thunder, then when the ship brought up and would naturally roll back to leeward, this immense, moving mass would meet and bring her up with a jerk, it seemed as if each roll was longer, heavier, and deeper than the one before. The impulse, that I have mentioned, was to make myself as light as possible, when she was rolling so that it seemed as if her yards must touch the water, and at the same time I must hold back and throw my weight on the opposite side. It is a very difficult sensation to describe and one intensely disagreeable to experience.

The Captain did not come to breakfast immediately and I thought Mrs. Whitmore looked and behaved as if she had something on her mind. When the Captain came in we found out what it was, for he informed us that he had turned about and was running for the Falkland Islands. Of course, both Julia and myself were astounded. The Captain, the officers and some of the men had been below and they were quite overcome with the look of things. Immense pipes were broken like pipestems and pipes and half-pipes even were to be seen in all sorts of queer positions; one pipe was imbedded in the side of the ship, another piece was standing upright in a case of crockery ware, and the whole mass was rolling, and turning and twisting about from side to side and fore and aft, it was not safe for the men to go down, they would venture just far enough to see the iron flying about and then come running up the ladder. It was found afterward that where pipes of an upper layer rolled and rubbed one against the pipes beneath them, grooves an inch deep were worn in the lower pipes by the ridges in the upper.

The Captain decided to make for the Falklands, as they were nearer and there would be a fair wind for that port, although he was not sure there would be facilities as suitable for reloading as at Rio.

40

Today has been a mixed, queer feeling day to us, we can't settle ourselves to our usual occupations. We felt that the trip will be prolonged beyond calculation, my California plans upset, and the people at home much worried, still it would not be safe to go on and I am thankful that we have a careful captain, as I think some would have gone on regardless of risk.

Sunday, March 27

Hardest days of all.

If we were facing this hurricane, as we should be if we had not turned back instead of running before it, I really think we should have rounded the Cape and only added to the number of those who are lost, no one knows how, at sea.

It seems to me, if a ship is well built and sea-worthy, there is much less danger from storms and gales than from the cargo; coals take fire, wheat and almost all general cargo will shift unless well stowed. We have been actually glued to our berths today except at meal times. While at dinner a terrific sea broke over us and torrents of water poured down upon the Captain, as he sat at the table, on the table and besprinkled us all generally. The baby was in his high-chair at his father's side, so he came in for his share of the ducking, we were all so surprised that no one thought of seizing upon and dragging him away, so he sat and took all that came to him, when it was all over he fairly howled.

The sea broke over the house and came in through the skylight, it wet the whole cabin pretty thoroughly, as the water had to be dipped up in my room and after cabin. Water was flying about so that the officers have to keep their watch on the house, instead of the quarter-deck as usual. Why they should have selected, for their promenade, that portion which covered my berth I can't say, but so it was and all night long the martial tread of Mr. Dow and the manly shuffle (due to rubber boots reaching to his hips) of Mr. Goodwin sounded above me, and extra scuffle and tramp just over my head and another at my feet as they turned about.

The gale subsided towards morning and Monday came in with fresh, fair wind and much less sea. The Captain hopes to sight the light on the Falklands by midnight; he has no chart, he will therefore have to signal for a pilot. We occupy ourselves in studying the *South Atlantic Sailing Directions* for descriptions of the islands and discussing the "square meal" of which we are to partake as soon as we land. We have already planned our first breakfast in San Francisco but we are

41

afraid the resources of Stanley will not furnish so elaborate a meal. Our menu, in consequence, has to be constantly altered; upon one thing Mrs. Whitmore and I are agreed and as it is a very modest desire, I should not be surprised if it were gratified. We are to have baked potatoes at every meal and as the *South Atlantic Sailing Directions* informs us that mutton and beef are both abundant and cheap as well as good, we have decided upon baked potatoes and beef-steak for our first repast. Julia and the Captain, less modest, require onions to complete their happiness. Speaking seriously, I feel that I would willingly sacrifice a good deal for a basket of fresh fruit and vegetables.

At midnight the Captain approached as near as he dared to the islands and then although a fresh, fair wind was blowing, he lay to till morning. This morning, Alas! a contrary wind springs up and a heavy current sets us off from the islands so we tack about all the morning.

Between two and three p.m. the pilot comes on board and, contrary to the appearance of the pilot in Philadelphia, he quite comes up to our idea of what a pilot should be. We all gather about him, the Captain, Mrs. Whitmore, the mate, Julia and myself, and proceed to ask him more questions than any one man could answer in days. According to his yarns, everything in the way of vegetables is to be had, but he is very doubtful about fruit, as there is cholera in Monte Video [Uruguay] and steamers do not touch there at present. There is no fruit raised on the islands, if we except one small crab-apple tree on the island (the tree, we afterwards learned, is a very old specimen in the Government gardens and has been carefully coddled by the different Governors down to the present time, the present Governor meeting with the above mentioned success. We saw the apple carefully preserved in alcohol).

Thus, before landing I saw my prospect of partaking of bananas and oranges growing beautifully less and farther away (we did manage to purchase a few oranges just before we left Stanley and while we were there we had some beautiful pears and apples sent us by Mrs. Dean, but that, with some lemons sent me, the night before we sailed, was the extent of our fruit eating experience in Stanley).

The island, we only see the East Falkland as we approach, looked lovely to see all the day, in tacking back and forth this morning we had many different views of it. The sea was warm and bright, so we were on deck most of the time, then after our rough weather it was delightful to have so little motion.

The island has not a tree or a bush upon it and as the town is at the head of a succession of reef-like harbors, with the exception of the lighthouse, no buildings were in sight, only conical hills or mountains, breaking out in all directions, and rocks everywhere. The comparatively level land was quite green and looked like some of our Maine pasture lands, minus the bushes; on account of this resemblance, heightened by the sun shining bright and clear as it does in our September I loved to look upon it, I did not know before there was so much beauty in barren pasture land.

The day we entered Stanley was celebrated in more ways than one. It was one of the very few days in the year when the wind did not blow; such days are rare and much valued, usually a strong wind, even gale, blows from sunrise to sunset.

The first day we went on shore was another windless day, perfectly lovely, warm and sunny. Julia and I went off in the steam launch with the Captain when he went to business, and spent the morning on shore. We forgot to watch whether it felt queer to be walking on land again, but we did notice the green lawns and flowers growing in great profusion and peculiar brilliancy, in the gardens and greenhouses. Every house in Stanley, I believe, has its greenhouses, tiny or large according to the means of the possessor; it was such a pleasure always to walk about the streets, for one saw lovely flowers at nearly every window. That morning we hung over all the fences and admired and sighed until we discovered some little pink and white English daisies growing in the green at the roadside; we then and there sat down and filled our hands. It was such a lovely morning that all Stanley, including the naval officers, was out; to say these good people stared would but faintly express it, however we sat still and picked our daisies.

That afternoon Mrs. Dean called upon us and the next day we had cards for an afternoon dancing party to be given early in the next week. From that time on the very hospitable people of Stanley seemingly devoted themselves to our entertainment and the tedium of our nine weeks sojurn in the Falklands was much lessened by their kindness.

As no pen of mine could do justice to the Falklands and as we really saw so little of the country, I propose to copy a few facts from our unfailing source of information, the *South Atlantic Sailing Directions*.

43

The Falkland Islands sit between fifty one degrees and fifty three degrees S. latitude and fifty seven degrees and sixty two degrees W. longitude and consist of two prinicipal islands, East and West Falklands, with many others of different sizes clustered about them. The greatest length of East Falkland is ninety five miles and greatest breadth fifty three miles, the West being smaller. There are about two hundred islands in all, all being deeply indented by sounds, bays, harbors, creeks, and rivulets, perhaps no spot in the world being so irregular in coast-line and so full of harbors and creeks. The sovereignty of the Falklands is vested in the British Crown and this local administration is conducted by a Governor who lives at Stanley. Formerly there was some question as to ownership of these islands, they being claimed by Spanish, French and English. They were discovered in August 1592 by John Davis but although successively claimed by the above mentioned countries, they remained unoccupied and unsettled until November 1820 when Commander Jewell took possession in the name of the Argentina Republic, this act was not known for several years in Europe. In 1829 some question regarding the seal fishers coming up between the settlers and the United States of North America, the colonials were seized by a captain of an American man-of-war and taken to Buenos Aires to attend trial. While discussing this question Great Britain stepped in and reasserted her claim; a few of the settlers returned to the island, but affairs were not prosperous and in August eight Indians attacked and killed the colonists, pillaged the houses, drove off the cattle and horses; a Mr. Brisbane was one of thebest-knownof the settlers. Nothing was known of this outrage until 1834, in this same year the first Governor was appointed. The old settlement at the head of Berkeley Sound was chosen for headquarters, and Port Louis was the name given to the settlement. Later on in 1842 the seat of the government was removed to Stanley Harbor. The prime feature in recent progress of the Falkland Islands is the occupation of East Falkland by a company called the Falkland Island Company. This company owns large tracts of land on the different islands where it has cattle ranches. The islands can hardly be considered interesting as to outward appearance, some portions of East Falkland being so low as to be hardly perceptible from ship five miles at sea. The West Falkland is more marked, some of the hills being between two thousand and three thousand feet above sea level. There are no trees and the only shrub that has as yet been known to thrive is called the "tea-plant" (which ordinary observers would term a vine growing quite as close to the ground as the cranberry at home), the leaves being used for making a [one word] termed tea. The berry of this plant is of a bright rose color and of quite an agreeable flavor. Peat of excellent quality exists everywhere, consequently there are peat-bogs in abundance. These islands have no native inhabitants or wild animals of any kind except rabbits and rats, but water fowl of many kinds are abundant, offering both amusement and good eating to the people of Stanley. Penguins contribute eggs in abundance and are considered a luxury, the Penguin Rookery being one of the showplaces of the islands. Fish are said to be very plentiful but we tasted only one variety which, both in looks and taste, resembled smelt. The country about Stanley can hardly be called level as there are elevations all about and towards the west end, between Stanley and the old settlement of Port Louis, there are very distinguished mountains, one being about two thousand feet. The country outside of the town is all called the "camp," as there are no roads and no trees for landmarks, no settlements are far apart, it requires no little experience to find one's way about this "camp." In walking in the camp near Stanley I came across what looked to me like a few tracks made by cattle, but was told that it was a trail leading to one of the settlements. The riding is very hard or it appears to be so to an onlooker, as I did not mount a horse, the riding season being over, I cannot speak from experience. The riders do not rise in the saddle as is usually the case in riding a trotting horse. The horses are very small. With exceedingly short legs they take very short steps, they strike a sort of dog trot which they keep up day in and day out, being very tough little animals. A gentleman assured me that he had frequently ridden sixty miles in a day. Such a thing as a buggy or carriage is quite unknown in Stanley, where there are the only respectable streets of the whole island. The weather is frequently stormy; the wind always blows and the roads always muddy, consequently, as the distances are for the most part great, it is something of an undertaking, arrayed in apparel suitable to the occasion, to take part in evening festivities. Such darkness I have rarely ever experienced and to make an evening expedition still more exciting the principle thoroughfare, esplanade, promenade, or whatever it may be called, follows the shore close to the water's edge in many places and has the most unexpected turns and twists in it. To add to the horrors the high iron railing, which formerely guarded the most exposed portion of the street, was carried away in a peat slip so that nothing hinders the unwary and the intoxicated from walking off into the water. We were frequently assured that it was almost impossible to save anyone who was unfortunate as to fall into the harbor, the water being so icy as to paralyze him almost immediately. The natives propose to know every turn, rock and pitfall in their street, so that darkness is no hindrance to their going about in safety and after being piloted through and over and around all difficulties several nights I learned to depend entirely upon my escort and take the night, with its varying degrees of darkness as the brightest day.

Some day I may be able to do partial justice to Stanley and its inhabitants by telling of our experiences there. I hope I may never be led to forget the people or the kindness lavished upon us and although I may never be able to repay them, I in turn may be able to succor some forlorn and homesick mortal stranded in like manner.

While in Stanley Julia and I changed state-rooms, the one I had been occupying being the much larger of the two, and it seemed only fair that she should have it the rest of the way. My present one, although smaller, is of much better shape and can be filled up much more satisfactorily. I found in Stanley a very pretty red satin splasher and valance for my washstand and covers for my lockers. I have fresh muslin with which to cover the red when we get into fine weather. With my wall-pockets, bright colored bags that I brought from home and a bunch of peacock's feathers, some Fuegian curiosities, a lamb-skin rug and a large bouquet of the most beautiful flowers, all sent off to me by friends in Stanley, my room looks very home-like and pretty. Add to these a porcelain shaded duplex burner brass lamp shining equally upon berth and a red-backed camp chair securely anchored beneath the one and beside the other and I think everyone would acknowledge that I have most comfortable quarters. I am constantly reminded of thoughtfulness and kindness of our friends in Stanley, of Mrs. Dean in particular, they having been back and forth between the Falklands and England until they know thoroughly what is most necessary for one's comfort on board ship. It seemed to me that I had been sufficient with every imaginable article large or small, from pens and boot buttons to books, before we left Stanley but the night before we sailed, the last time the launch came out to us there came four large boxes and packages to me, all filled with eatables and keepsakes of all kinds. The beautiful flowers lasted a week or more, just the time I needed them most for I was a little seasick at first; the large tin of tea cakes, two weeks or more, the fruit that Mrs. Dean had managed to get somewhere lasted still longer, and the wine, English biscuit and [1 word] will furnish us with dessert and stolen repasts for sometime to come.

We sailed from Stanley the twenty sixth of May, late in the afternoon and before long we were fairly settled on board ship. It takes so long to pack away shore garments and get out and stow away the clothing necessary for the voyage, all sorts of weather must be provided for.

I should be very proud to say that I was not sea-sick, but Alas! on the twenth seventh we struck a head-wind and a Cape Horn roll and I succumbed, it really seemed as if I had not been to sea at all. I was much afraid of repeating my North Atlantic experience so I determined not to give up until my room was settled, the consequence was that I packed away a few things or drove a few tacks and then vomited, made fast some moveable object and vomited again. I kept this up until after dinner and had vomited seven or eight times, when everything being pretty well settled I gave in and made myself comfortable in my berth. I did not vomit after that day but I cling in pretty closely to my berth for two or three days, and indeed with the ship rolling and plunging about so, one's berth is the only really safe and comfortable place.

It is much harder, not only for one's stomach, but in every way, coming out into such rough seas and stormy weather than working into them gradually. Before turning back we were in Lat. fifty six degrees twenty one minutes S. and Long. sixty five degrees seventeen minutes W. and had encountered very heavy gales, but I had not had a touch of sea-sickness. One thing consoled Julia and myself much, Mrs. Whitmore was quite sick one day; we thought if she, with her fifteen years experiences suffered, what could be expected of us.

Another disagreeable part of coming out in such weather is the necessity of making everything tight and fast, everything moveable must be braced or lashed and as our long stay on shore had made us forgetful of ship life, we learn by painful experience that it takes a powerful amount of tacking to make things secure. The second night, in the midst of my disagreeable feelings, I was conscious, said consciousness adding much to my unhappiness, that things were moving about in my room in a very lively manner. In the morning I found my chair flat on the floor, my underclothing scattered about, every drawer in the locker stretched to its utmost capacity, and everything generally mixed up, I managed to right things a little and tumbled back into bed disgusted enough. Of seasickness I think I can now write as one who knows whereof she writheth. My experience has been that it is not worse than the nausea which visits me frequently at home, when I have been having a severe pain in my eyes or suffering from any severe pain. As a cure there is absolutely nothing like eating, eating constantly and eating long, no matter how sick you are or how many times your stomach turns a somersault during the process, eat fast and as much as you can, when you can bear no more, rush to your berth and lie flat on your back. Don't let the stomach get empty for it only weakens in consequence and is liable to retain food, therefore I say again Eat, Eat, Eat. I had had this remedy preached on the occasion of my other attack, the Captain, Mrs. Whitmore, and the steward were all urging and insisting upon my eating, but I simply could not bring myself to it, or I thought I could not, the consequence was that I was very much sicker than I was this time.

For more than two weeks after leaving Stanley the history of one day would do for all, head winds and heavy roll, or if we managed to gain a little one day, we were sure to lose it later on. When we had been out eleven days the Captain informed us that we could run back to the Falklands in one day if we should turn about. I knew we were making nothing so asked no questions and did not wish to be told just how badly off we were, but sometimes knowledge was thrust upon us.

It had always been a mystery to me, when I heard people tell of spending weeks and months getting round the Cape, how they could put in so much time in going such a short distance. I suppose they were constantly encountering hurricanes and that their lives were in danger from morning till night and right till morning, and that was why that part of the voyage was so much dreaded. The mystery is now explained, and much more also that was mysterious about a sea voyage.

The difficulty in rounding the Cape from the Atlantic side is that there is almost always a westerly, or a wind related to a westerly wind, blowing, and a very heavy current from the larger and more powerful Pacific to be encountered. Some winds of a westerly direction may be from such an angle that some southing may be gained, and it is quite an object to get far enough south to clear the Cape, the luck in, in taking advantage of every wind that is not a head wind to get this amount of southing, or as the Captain expresses it, "in a position" to round the Cape, then after a long succession of winds from the opposite quarter, an easterly wind is almost sure to set in for a few hours and round you go; if the east wind comes before you are in a position it does very little good, for the dreaded Cape must be given a wide berth, there must be no chances taken in that direction consequently the ship must be tacked; oftentimes after a ship is "in position" instead of the desired east wind, a strong head wind or gale sets in and she is driven back and far out of her course. After you round the Cape ever constant warfare must be constantly waged in order that you may not lose what has been gained. One is not considered out of danger until he has reached fifty degrees S. on the Pacific side.

Considering the gales and hurricanes from the contrary and the zephyrs from the favorable quarter, it is not to be wondered at if we began to think we were destined to pass our lives between 50 degrees and 60 degrees S. latitude. However all things must end and on the evening of the tenth of June the wind took a turn in our favor and the next morning between nine and ten we sighted the Cape. It was a very dark, cloudy, misty sort of a day, the cabin was not out of twilight for the day, but the brightest sunshine could not have made it look more cheerful or our hearts lighter.

I spent the greater part of the morning on deck; I would stay as long as I could bear the cold and wet then make a dive for the cabin stove and get thawed out. Sighting land at sea has always a great fascination for me, and on this occasion so happy were we in getting on that even the bleak, rocky, barren peaks of Cape Horn were lovely. I got several salt-water duckings in my devotion to the view, and indeed we were fortunate, for the Captain says that in fifteen years he has not had such a look at the detested Cape and Mrs. Whitmore had never before seen it distinctly, almost always through in a fog hanging about it and the neighboring islands. The Captain says there is something very peculiar and unmistakable about the shape of the island, but I could not see that it differed in any way from the islands about or from Staten Land, unless if it were possible it were a little more forlorn and melancholy, if it were not land, beloved land, the sight of the cold, bleak, snow-covered peaks would give me a fit of the blues. Until afternoon we were constantly opening up and passing islands similar in size and shape to Cape Horn, but we were nearer the latter than either of the others, we were about four miles from the Cape. At about four p.m. we sighted Il de Fonso, the last bit of land we had to fear, if only we were not blown back. We passed between it and the mainland and hoped we had seen the last of it when the night shut down upon us.

All this day we have had just wind enough to have what the officers call "pretty sailing." During the voyage I have spent hours on the poop-deck, clinging to the safety bar in front of the wheel-house, from which position we can see the full length of the ship. The Captain is as fond of the sight as I and always calls upon me to share his enjoyment. When she is more enchanting than usual, we are always sure of one or more salt water baths in our zeal but we do not mind. Whatever else may happen on this somewhat despairing and disastrous voyage I am sure I shall not lose my fondness for the ship that has so far taken us safely through so many dangers. For there is no doubt but that, if the ship had not been well built and without a flaw, we should have come to grief long before this, our cargo is of such an unmanagable nature. The Captain and the carpenter have been and are still keeping careful watch, the carpenter spending hours each day in the hold, it is his first thought in the morning and his last at night.

After enjoying such a run of luck nothing more could be expected, for it has been our experiences for the entire voyage, that one day of favorable wind must be followed by weeks of head wind or calms and that night the wind died out and the next morning Il de Fonso was still in sight and nearer apparently than when I took leave of it at sundown the night before. How we ever managed to leave it behind is a mystery, for days we had no wind and a strong current was setting towards the island.

Off Cape Horn, in the region of perpetual gales and storms, in mid-winter--and doldrums, doldrums. The Captain has said "I never experienced anything like this before" until he quite wore out saying and we hearing it. For nearly a week the ocean was as calm and we felt as little motion as in the tropics. We seized the opportunity to make up a quantity of candy, for we did not leave Stanley as well stocked as we did Philadelphia, for the candy of Stanley we did not pine. One great drawback to our happiness being the fact that the hens had suddenly struck and we had absolutely not one egg with which to use the confectioners sugar brought from home. We besought the carpenter to use his influence with the hens and begged the steward to feed them with meat and vegetables, but all to no good, and if Mrs. Whitmore had not finally managed to come across one in her upper bureau drawer, I do not know what we should have done. We devoted ourselves to our favorite kinds, walnut creams for the Captain, peppermint drops for Mrs. Whitmore, fig paste for Julia, molasses for me and two or three other kinds as experiments. We thought we had made enough to last weeks, but a very few days finished off the lot, with the exception of the Captain's and my stock, the Captain locking his up, and mine not being much of a success as candy but very fair gingerbread; ours as I say lasted some time.

We also devoted ourselves to experiment in cooking during this calm time. I really did not know so many nice things could be made without eggs; we were very successful with molasses cookies and gingerbread, but our sugar cookies, attempted on account of the Captain's fondness for them, with the exception of one sheet, went overboard before they were baked. We also invented two new ways of preparing the canned oysters, made goose-berry jam, blueberry pies and apple turnovers. The steward rather frowned upon our efforts in these lines as it encroached upon his domain, so we do not dare trust to his care in the galley, consequently Axel is in constant demand, and he does very well for us, watching carefully while in the oven and stirring faithfully when on the stove. As he is so strong that we get him to do all the beating on our cake and gingerbread and he makes good suggestions sometimes when we are at a loss how to proceed. We have also discovered that bread toasted by ourselves at the stove in the forward cabin is much nicer than bread toasted, until it is both hard and dry, by the steward in the galley and then brought to the table cold. We began by taking turns at the toasting-fork but very soon Axel came to toast as well as we and at last the steward got it through his celestial brain that bread toasted long and hard and black did not make the best toast. Our last two and happiest experiments and these with gingerbread best fair to be favorites for the rest of the trip, were graham rolls or muffins and beans baked a la New England instead of a la Chinese. When I first thought of this trip and was told that, on board ship baked beans were served twice a week for dinner and warmed over for supper on those days my soul shuddered within me, for to mind the beans and possible thunder showers would very nearly offset the possible pleasure to be experienced. However, I decided to take the chances and here I am now looking forward, nay even pining for Tuesdays and Fridays (bean days) and not contented even. I prepare a special dish for the benefit of our table on Saturday nights and Sunday mornings, and some weeks, when not entirely overcome with shame, another pot in the middle of the week. Such luck is my fallen state!!! I even look forward with joy to getting up on the mornings when we have beans for breakfast, and with anguish on off mornings. What a perpetual diet of beans will do for me I do not know, but as I seem to be gaining in flesh all the time, I shall continue them for awhile.

The evenings of these days we, Julia and I, beguile with cards, bezique, when the ship is sufficiently steady for us to manage a quantity of cards, cribbage at other times and always as a grand finale, a few games of cut-throat euchre, Mrs. Whitmore taking a hand at this. It is a great trial to us that the Captain not only does not know one card from another, but will not be induced to learn. We could have an unlimited number of games of whist if only he would live up to his opportunities. Bezique being a game newly taken up we devote our time principally to it, bracing ourselves on my berth when we cannot sit at the table comfortably. We have been known on particularly dull days to spend the whole afternoon and part of the evening at it. In consequence of this devotion our match games at cribbage advance very slowly, as I was ahead at last accounts, I don't see but that I am sure of one square meal on our arrival at San Francisco. What makes this matter doubly sure Julia not only brought away her U. S. paper money from the Falklands but quite a supply of English shillings, and I am, as usual, quite penniless, also in debt.

Our refreshments on these evenings can hardly be looked upon as elaborate or [one word], being peppermint and water. We verily have come to such a pass that we look upon lumps of sugar soaked in peppermint and water as the height of luxury and the most satisfactory of drinks after the sugar has all been eaten. When it was found necessary to replenish the bottle from a large flask that was supposed to be well filled imagine our feelings, our anguish even, when it was discovered that this bottle was also nearly empty.

We have been preparing ourselves to resign many cherished articles of diet but we imagined we had peppermint enough to last us round the world, consequently we have used it freely at all seasons, even wasted it. Our voyage promises to be prolonged to such an unusual extent that we must necessarily run short of some things not procurable in Stanley; we shall not want for necessaries, but it is quite a new and not altogether pleasant experience to find one's self running out of some simple and heretofore considered indisposable article. We have an unpleasant habit of what the Captain calls "running a thing to death." If one of us suddenly discovers that something is particularly palatable eaten or cooked in a certain new way, we all immediately adopt that method and we are not satisfied with having it occasionally, but no, we must partake thereof at all seasons and times, the consequence is we wear the thing out and never want to taste it again in any shape. In that way we lose one article from our somewhat limited bill of fare. There were two unfortunate facts in connection with the peppermint; we had not commenced our run on it when we were in Stanley, so we had not discovered that we were short or we could have laid in a new supply; second we had not yet tired of it when the supply gave out.

Another luxury that we have watched with anxious and longing eyes as it slowly but surely melted away, crumbled perhaps would be the more correct expression, is our spruce gum, such a comfort as it has been to us. I rarely chew it at home but took a small package with me but this stock gave out long ago and no words could or can now express my gratitude to Miss Beaumont, when on opening a mysterious package presented by her with the words "a very [two words] game but one I hope you will enjoy." I had several of these delightful packages given me just as I was leaving home, to be opened at different stages of the voyage, but this was the last, as I say, my delight was extreme when I discovered that this good sized box contained gum. I was then on my last piece and had made up my mind and mouth to the deprivation for the rest of the voyage. Hence the discovery brought great relief and much joy to the entire family and the united thanks were immediately voted to Miss Beaumont.

It has been great fun for us to watch the baby through the rough weather. He is a very active little fellow so it is very hard to keep him from creeping about even when Mrs. Whitmore considers it quite unsafe for him to be on the floor but however he manages it he never gets upset. We are all floundering about and often times almost losing our footing but he bends this way and that, suiting his body to the motion of the ship, even in his high chair when it seems as if he must have a fall, as he persists in standing up unless tied down, he always manages to balance himself. His dexterity in this respect is only equalled by his capacity for recovering large pieces of bread, crackers, and foreign substances of all kinds (he puts everything in his mouth) that are apparently choking him. He sometimes cries if the object is hard and rough but he is never frightened and coughs away until he gets it up. Any other child would be choked dozens of times. I assure his mother that she need never worry for he is bound to be hung.

In running from one subject to another I have rather

wandered from my text. In speaking of the weather off Cape Horn, taking into consideration what we were led to expect and what we actually experienced, I am convinced, not only of that part of the voyage but of all, that not the gales and storms (for however fierce and disagreeable they are usually of short duration) but the discomfort, unavoidable in ship life in cold weather, are the real drawbacks to a sea voyage.

A ship however well and newly built can never be thoroughly heated so that one has to become accustomed to a certain amount of cold, for in rough weather it is not safe to sit near the stove and to stand by it one has to be pretty well braced, then to get the greatest amount of heat coal must be the fuel used and that always means more or less coal gas, decidedly more when the wind is dead aft. At times we begged for wood, for smoke although unpleasant is not deadly poisonous. I know I never was so cold for so long in my life as I was during the months we spent off Cape Horn, and yet the mercury never went much below forty degrees above zero, but it was a penetrating, clammy sort of a cold. Still, notwithstanding the drawback, we bore all our trials, with a few exceptions, bravely and cheerfully.

This has been, in many respects, an exceptional and disastrous voyage to the Whitmores and I think Mrs. Whitmore is sometimes almost superstitious. In all the twenty-five years of the Captain's sea-going life, this is the first time he has had to put in, he was never so long rounding the Horn, never had such a miserable apology for a steward or in many respects such inefficient officers, and naturally following, such a troublesome crew.

Our stay in Stanley was lengthened four or five weeks through the misbehavior of our crew, one watch mutinied forty-eight hours before we reached the islands and the other knocked off work as soon as we were anchored. An attempt was made to bring them to terms, six of the Irish ring-leaders were taken on shore, tried, and sentenced to three weeks hard labor and imprisonment, the other nine were kept in close confinement on board ship and as most of them were Germans, a German officer came off from Stanley to labor with them, but all to no good. They were offered every inducement to remain with the ship; they had no complaint to make, they said they were treated well, had their full rations and of the best quality, they could only say "they must go with the crowd." Even Murphy, the ring-leader of all, had only the feeble excuse that the Captain called him a ring-leader. The Captain therefore was obliged to go to Valparaiso [Chile] for a new crew and we were left to wear away the time as best we could in Stanley, our souls harrowed by the thought that the ship was not ready to sail and the weather getting worse all the time.

One old fellow, belonging to the crew, a red-headed Irishman, Sullivan by name, deserves special mention. Until the new crew came he was the oldest man on board ship. When asked if he were willing to stay he asked if he should receive the same treatment that he had been receiving and being assured that he would, he said "I will stay" and stay he did and he chuckled much and long when on rowing us ashore one morning he saw his fellow countrymen at work getting out gravel, guarded by an armed policeman. When the new crew came his pay was raised and he was promoted to office of boatswain, what that office is or what its duties I have yet to learn, but he now takes his meals with the second mate and carpenter in the cabin instead of on his knees in the fo'castle.

Several of the men had received especially kind treatment from the Captain or some of us, one in particular, a German whom we called "Rudolph," not knowing his last name. I took much interest in him from the fact that he was very sick on coming out from Philadelphia. At intervals I would hear the Captain mention a sick man also much discussion as to proper medicine, I think Dr. Warren was consulted equally on his and my behalf, his was not an attack of sea-sickness however.

After the usual remedies had been applied to his case and he was rapidly growing worse, in the midst of my own misery I suddenly bethought myself of a simple but powerful remedy which, with others was suggested to me just before leaving home. The medicine was prepared and given him and after a little he was much better.

Later on we saw him crawling about the main deck and one day the Captain took me out to see him, Mrs. Whitmore giving me a glass of jelly to present to him, he thanked me with tears in his eyes and talked a little with us, using very good language, of course somewhat broken and with an accent, he also wrote a very good hand and he always selected a better class of books when he came with some of the others on Sunday mornings to solicit reading, but this was later.

During our convalescence I sent him portions of the soup that was put aside for my supper, soup being almost the only article of food that I could take, and we both seemed to thrive on it for we were soon out on deck, he pulling at the ropes and I in my hammock. He always seemed grateful and was always very polite and ready to do us any little service and we felt we could speak to him when he was about the quarter deck and be sure he would not take advantage. We also supposed he owed his recovery to the treatment we had given him but when asked what complaint he had to offer he said, "They did not give him any medicine when he was sick, the second mate gave him something that cured him." The German officer, who came off to talk with the men, declared this same Rudolph to be the very worst of the lot. Thus departed what little faith I had ever placed in sailors. Just before leaving the ship Rudolph came aft with some books which he gave me with a very pretty little prepared speech, thanking me for my kindness, etc. My never ceasing regret is that I did not then and there open the vials of my wrath and pour their contents upon his devoted head, but the mate was near by and I restrained myself.

Nothing touches a sailor so much as limiting the quantity of his medicines, he is not particular as to quality, anything bad tasting will do, only its healing qualities are in direct ratio to the vileness of the taste and the quantity administered. Castor oil and epsom salts are the favorites and are considered penance for all ills. When I first came out I nearly lost my breakfast one morning from meeting the Captain bearing a cup half filled with oil and getting a strong whiff of the sauce. The next moment I saw a sailor at the door smacking his lips and an empty cup in his hand. They scorn the use of peppermint or cinnamon as taste deadners, they love the pure, unadulterated castor oil taste. Three quarters of a cup of salts is considered a fair dose, Axel insisted upon administering a full cup on one occasion notwithstanding my protestations. They adore mustard plasters and are not satisfied if they have not raw, blistered places to show the next day.

All of which leads me to remark that a sailor is a queer animal, I really think he has the honor of occupying the lowest round of the ladder and upon his face is the seal of degradation; an intelligent brute would be insulted with such a companion. He is lazy, unscrupulous, one lying and the rest swearing to it, one stealing, the rest backing him, apparently not susceptible to kindness in the slightest degree. When on shore a slave to drink and the boarding-house keepers, at sea only recognizing as officer those who knock and bully them about, ready at any and all times to follow blindly the lead of one of his fellows who happens to be more unscrupulous and of a slightly stronger mind.

If we had not been forced to put into the Falklands there would have been no trouble with the men. When first coming out of Philadelphia there was some little difficulty, one watch refusing to wash down the decks at four a.m. when ordered, and once or twice afterwards one or two were saucy and they were all logged; if we had gone on, they would have behaved so well at the Cape and on the Pacific side that in all probability the Captain would have paid them off in San Francisco and said nothing.

They decided to run no risks however and mutinied, they had no money due them for there had been a large advance paid in Philadelphia and many had drawn largely from the slop chest. All this aided much to the Captain's embarrassment for he had to keep them and pay charges on shore and finally their fare to Sandy Point, if there had been anything due them he could have drawn upon it to help defray expenses. However the entertainment offered them on board ship was not elaborate, for after they refused work, the chief of their diet was bread and their only drink water. As the authorities of Stanley would not have them landed there they had to be sent on to the nearest port (this is a law) and Sandy Point or Punta Arenas in the Straits of Magellan was the first spot where they could be landed by permission of the authorities. The inhabitants of that small colony bitterly regretted their advent, for they were like so many wild animals let loose, they supposed they were going on to Valparaiso and were much disgusted when they and their belongings were dumped in that out-of-the-way spot. They evidently considered that the people owed them a living, for they not only demanded contributions of everyone they met but in some cases used violence. When the Captain returned from Valparaiso he learned that they had become such a terror to the peaceful colonists that the women of the settlement did not dare venture out, and that some of them had been imprisoned and others sent out of the country.

The Captain brought a new crew back from Valparaiso with him and he had to be continually on the watch lest one or more of them escape at some of the landing places; to add to his misery the captain and officers of both steamers were German and the passengers were either Spanish or Germans and above all German food was served, the Captain loathing the German style of cooking. In consequence of all these trials he came home quite worn out and looking badly.

The logging to which I referred takes the place of the ancient flogging and is the one redress possessed by the Captain and it is furnished him by law. For the law lately revised is entirely for the protection of the sailors and takes the punishment of mutinies or disobedient crews out of the hands of the

57

officers. If "revenge is sweet" I suppose it does as well in the end, but it is hard for the innocent to suffer with the guilty as would assuredly happen if a gale should come up while the men were practicing any of their little tricks, as when we were two days out from Stanley and the second mate's watch refused to work.

An English ship came into Stanley ten days after we arrived, it had been disabled in the same gale as we but they could have kept on their course to Liverpool if the sailors had not refused to work and forced the captain to put into Stanley, thus giving themselves two or three months longer pay, endangering the captain's position (for he felt sure he would be turned away on his arrival in Liverpool) and forcing the owners to pay four times the ordinary cost of repairs. There was really no danger in going on either, for they had passed the Cape and were almost sure of good weather the rest of their passage.

I have shown how much our troubles were increased by the behavior of our first crew. When there is any trouble at sea, the names of the men causing the outbreak are taken, entered into the log and their offense, as the trouble is usually between the officers and men, the Captain hears both sides of the story, questioning the men carefully, the defense is then entered in the log. On the arrival of the ship at the port to which she is bound, officers and men go before a court and the case stated, there is oftentimes a long trial, the judge decides whether the men shall be fined or imprisoned or the officers fined. If a captain has what is called a "fighting mate" there is no logging aboard that ship, but if the captain should see his mate strike another man, he would either have to keep out of sight on his arrival in port or else be fined or perhaps imprisoned.

Oftentimes the men, instigated and backed by the boarding house keepers, complain of bad treatment and are prepared to go into court and swear to any number of lies. The captain either allows the case to go on or administers bribes to the boarding house masters and/or stops proceedings.

Our mate is not a fighting character it is needless to state, on the contrary, he is the most lamb-like creature alive, much to my disgust for I should like to have seen a few of the men well thrashed.

June 22

Today we really start on our westward course, having

58

reached fifty degrees S. latitude we may consider the Cape safely rounded. It is nearly four weeks since we left Stanley, this may be considered hard luck, we hoped to be in San Francisco in two months from the time we left Stanley. Alas! for our expectations.

June 27

We have swept through the "Roaring Forties" in four days, the best run of luck we have had since coming out, and for which we are proportionately grateful. We are followed by swarms of Cape pigeons, hens and albatross and such a greedy set of followers were never seen. I feed them mornings with bits of bread, saved for me by the steward, and one whole afternoon the Captain and I devoted to feasting them upon the contents of the "slush pot." Slush, being an accumulation of all the waste grease in the ship, is a decidedly necessary, ill-smelling mess and far from pleasant to look upon. The disagreeable part we forgot, so intent were we in watching the manuvers of the birds. The hens and albatross did not venture very near the ship, but the pigeons were all about, flying, swimming and diving in their eagerness to obtain small portions of the filth which they adore. They are utterly fearless, facing the heavy spray thrown from the stern of the ship and the largest albatross with equal courage. The Captain and I took great delight in waiting for heavy seas that we might watch the little things dive into the depths for morsels of the slush. The pigeons are always of the same size, the same shape and same color even to the spots on the wings of each, black and white as to color, the plummage's grebelike in texture and the wings are very long and wide for the size of the bird. At first it was a mystery what they did with so much wing when swimming, but like the albatross they shut their wings up like a double jointed jack knife and make themselves into very compact and muscular little birds.

The Cape hens are very pretty, half as large again as the pigeons and of different shades of brown, they are slender and much more graceful. I would like to have had the wings and breast of one but was not willing to fish for one with salt pork and a fish-hook, it seemed too cruel when they were apparently so happy. My experience with the logger-head duck skins sent off to me by Mr. Hardy of Stanley did not encourage me to attempt the care of any more skins. The albatross is the ugliest and most ungainly of all water birds. I am utterly disappointed in him; like that of the Southern Cross, his fame

59

has far outstripped the reality. All these birds adopt and follow a ship for days and weeks, even months if the weather
continues cold enough; where or when they sleep no one knows
for seemingly they always are at hand and always keep their
number, perhaps like the albatross, they sleep on the wing.
Furnishing food for the birds is not the only use to which the
slush pot is put on board ship, it and the tar-pot go hand in
hand, for without this grease the men could not handle the tar
for any length of time. It also provides the Captain with one
of his favorite stories, for he cites, as illustration of the
strength of a sailor's stomach, the case of the man who
spread his bread with slush, the older and stronger the better
he liked it. A slight reference to this yarn, during rough
weather, was apt to bring on a fit of sea-sickness, if one was
inclined that way.

June 29

We have been congratulating ourselves on escaping a gale
in the forties only to be overtaken by a hurricane in thirty
eight degrees S. latitude. Such a disagreeable day as it has
been, the officers and men having no dinner and we three
eating ours an hour or two later than usual. Late in the afternoon the Captain said he could eat a sandwich if it were
passed out to him; Axel was needed on deck so we made
sandwiches, prepared whiskey for the men, took care of the
baby and crawled about as best we could. One can hardly stir
these rough days that some of the family does not call out
"look out, be careful," etc. The Whitmores are so afraid that
we shall be thrown down and hurt in some way, and indeed a
broken bone would be no joke at sea, I have never been thrown
down, but I must say I have been brought up pretty suddenly
by the side of the cabin.
The wind subsiding and the sea fueling the effect of the
oil dropped upon its troubled surfaces, peace was somewhat
restored by night and dinner was served at the usual supper
hour. Through all the tumult the baby has been perfectly
furious because he has not been allowed to crawl about on the
cabin floor as usual.
Our new crew is indeed a motly set, with names as diversified as their nationalities, and I never knew names so ap-
plicable. One man, very tall and lean with a very fair
washed-out sort of countenance, rejoices in the name of Blue.
Another, with round, full face, cross-eyed with a few scatter-
ing side whiskers of a dull straw color, bears, of all names in

the world, that of Moon. "Moon up in the sky" as he told the Captain when Captain Whitmore looked a little incredulous on being told his name. Another with a refined face and the most languishing brown eyes, with a nose beyond reproach, adorns or is adorned by the aristocratic name of Finnisia. According to the Captain this last individual is one of the most abandoned of the lot.

I have no doubt there are other names quite as appropriate, but my acquaintance thus far has been limited to those who come aft for medicines. For coming from so hot a climate as Valparaiso into such severe weather has completely doubled them up, as the Captain expresses it. There they lead such disolute lives on shore that it takes them weeks to recover from the effects. Such an assortment of boils, cracked hands, salt water sores, and so many attacks of Cape Horn fever has seldom been known. Fryers balsam, flax-seed poultices, mutton tallow and castor oil have been in constant demand. I have poulticed, salved, and tried all sorts of experiments with all sorts of afflictions, but have finally come back to flax-seed and mutton tallow as infallible remedies.

How such a battered, wizened, undersized set of men ever managed to get the ship round the Cape, I cannot imagine. As usual the mate managed to get all the decent men in his watch, how it happens that the lame, the halt and the blind as well as the Fuegians fall to the second mate's there is beyond us to imagine. As Mr. Dow is a constitutional growler and nagger the Captain thinks he selects his watch with an eye to the men least likely to rise up and thrash him, if this is his aim he shows much discrimination.

The one colored man of the lot is a character and he affords us constant amusement and excitement, there surely never was another such a lazy darky. I can't blame the men for delighting to tease him, he moves about so slowly, there is a constant temptation to stumble over him and tread upon his heels, his blood-curdling howls, uttered at the slightest provocations, add to their enjoyment. At first these sudden yells, especially if heard at night, fairly made our scalps rise from our heads, but now we pay no attention unless there promises to an unusually interesting encounter, when we all hasten to the scene of action; the Captain rather sympathizes with the darky, so he always rushes to the rescue.

Our most interesting combat has been between the bo'swain, a big red-headed Irishman and the man of color. We heard yells, howls and incoherent stuttering mixed with oaths loud and deep in a decidedly Irish accent, whether there were blows or not we could not tell; by the time the Captain

61

arrived the darky was so beside himself with rage as to be utterly unintelligible but Mr. Sullivan so far recovered himself as to remark "I can bear a good deal, Captain, but I won't stand being damned by a nigger," and pitched in again, the Captain finally dragged off the darky.

As soon as he begins to yell the men let him alone and just flee the spot, for such hair-raising howls are sure to bring the whole ship out, they are his sole weapon for defense, but in a position like this, a whole arsenal of modern artillery would be as nothing in comparison.

Besides being lazy this South American negro knows absolutely nothing about a ship, he has been twice disrated and is now on boy's wages, even these he does not earn. He had a little trick of throwing himself violently on the deck and of being disabled for days in consequence, but after repeating this little trick two or three times, the Captain came up with him by forbidding the cook to issue his rations unless he were on deck. The cook was equal to the occasion and when the darky appeared at the galley door one morning and asked for his breakfast, cook replied "I no see you work, when I see you work, I give breakfast."

July 4

There is little besides the date to remind us that this is the "bright and glorious" Fourth, no ringing of bells, no firing of cannons to disturb our peaceful slumbers, no firecrackers and blessed fact! no fish horns to harrow our souls. I have never been in the habit of celebrating the day in a very reckless manner, but I have always been within the sound of some slight attempts at celebrating and with the gaieties of last year to look back upon, the day seems very quiet and unfourth-like. The difference, for we are still wearing our Cape Horn dress, my blue flannel has given place to my green tramping dress to be sure, but otherwise there has been no change. Axel indeed indulged in a rite the sailors take much stock in, whether to any good remains to be seen. He threw overboard this morning a pair of well worn rubber boots remarking as he made the sacrifice "Here's for three weeks to San Francisco and when we get there I will give you something else." I think we shall all be ready by that time to make heavy donations.

Passed "Robinson Crusoe Island," Juan Fernandez today, but five hundred fifty miles to westward of it. It is in the same latitude as Valparaiso, thirty three degrees seventeen minutes south latitude but five hundred miles west of it. Judging from the description in the *Sailing Directions*, it must be a more desirable place of refuge than the Falklands, the scenery being described as beautiful and the climate in every way desirable, but of course it is much too near Valparaiso for it to have facilities for refilling ships.

The Cape pigeons lately have been reinforced by four or five Carey's chickens, these little birds look very tiny in comparison with the pigeons and albatross, they appear perfectly at ease however, flying about among the other birds and attending strictly to their own affairs, whatever their object in life may be they carefully conceal it from us mortals. They are evidently tireless for I have never seen one at rest or even swimming on the water, but always flying about, unceasingly, occasionally skimming the water lightly with the tip of the wings or feet. They are a very tiresome bird to watch but rather interesting.

July 5

Today we have been much disturbed in our minds, two members of our family being on the sick list. At noon Mrs. Whitmore called me to look at Mr. Goodwin's hand, that he had some sort of lame hand I had heard from the Captain but had not thought of its being serious. The first look quite frightened me, another such a swollen, discolored looking member I had never seen. To me it looked like a very malignant type of erysipelas, more especially as the first indication of trouble had been a slight swelling or pimple; now some portions were of a dark angry red, others black, and all badly swollen. After a careful consultation with Dr. Warren, although he gave no instance of erysipelas in the hand, we decided to treat it as if it were that. For, if it should prove to be a carbuncle this treatment would do no harm, while the poultice for carbuncle would be worst possible for erysipelas. Having only a small box of homeopathic medicines and none of them suitable I was obliged to resort to the allopathic medicine chest. I gave large doses of quinine and kept the hand soaked in alcohol, continuing this treatment through the night.

Meanwhile the baby, who had been ailing all day, seemed decidedly worse and the rain and wind coming on the day shut down gloomily enough. We decicded to try homeopathic treatment for baby, as there is nothing like variety, and as he seemed to have taken cold, was feverish and had apparently a very sore throat, we gave him a hot bath and alternate doses of aconite and belladona. Mr. Goodwin being unable to keep his watch the Captain had to be on deck, as he did not like to trust the bo'swain, so we three females were left alone below and forlorn enough we felt.

The next morning both patients were a little better, Mr. Goodwin had had a wakeful night, the pain only easing off at every fresh application of alcohol. There was much less inflammation and we decided there was no erysipelas, consequently flax-seed poultices were ordered to the front. For more than a week, three times each day I made and applied these poultices but unlike most nurses, after it was once lanced, with the exception of one glance I did not even look at it, the glance sufficed, I never saw anything like it, the core seemed to extend up into the palm of the hand and it required days of constant poulticing to bring it out, the opening of the sore was on the side of the hand almost at the wrist.

The baby's sickness we afterwards traced to his teeth, as after a day or two the point of a large double tooth was visible and a day or two later another made its appearance. It is so hard to nurse a sick baby and doubly so on board ship, for we had nothing with which to tempt his appetite; I really felt very much worried about him one day, he would not taste food and the only way to make him take a thing was to hold his hands and feet and force the gruel down his throat. Axel is devoted to him and concocted some sort of a Swedish dish and was much pleased when the baby ate part of a cup. A little more than a week's time saw our invalids both much better.

Meanwhile this ship had put off her fine raiment and on her old clothes, for unlike most ladies she reserves her newest garments for bad weather. Just how patched and weather beaten the sails now bent really were I did not realize until remarking upon the poverty stricken appearance of those on a ship near us, I was informed that ours were exactly as bad, only we did not see them with the light shining through them.

We are within the tropics now but the weather remains rather colder than we like. Twenty three and one half degrees being the limit N. and S. of the sun's journey he must now be not far from his northern limit, but on his journey south, and our hottest weather will be on the other side of the line, yet it must be warmer soon. As it is, if we are careful to select a sheltered spot we are able to sit out with our sewing and on Sunday we spent the forenoon in our hammocks.

The Captain and carpenter between them have invented a new arrangement for our hammocks and at present we have them on the house in the most sheltered position, later on our souls or bodies will be pining for the most breezy spot, then we shall have an awning spread and if there is a zephyr the house will be the place to feel it.

The "arrangement" alluded to resembles nothing in the world so much as a large four-posted bed stead, minus the slats, made of heavy wood and carefully wedged at the corners; the hammocks are strung from bars at the head and foot and are side by side, very conveniently placed for reading aloud and altogether very comfortable.

July 15

Cries of "whale, whale ho!" have been sounding about the ship all day. This morning I was busy in my room and in the afternoon too comfortable in my hammock to disturb my self, consequently I did not get a full view of their mysteries. Mrs. Whitmore and Julia chased them all the afternoon and at night said they felt and were as tired as if they had been chasing a circus.

Jill(??), our darky, also spent the most of his time watching and making remarks in an audible undertone for my benefit, he was supposed to be giving his attention to a rail which he had been ordered to paint, although the mate's eye was upon him and his voice constantly reminding him of his duty, by careful calculation, he was twenty minutes painting four feet of an inch wide rail on one side and the edge, at the end of that time he had worked out of my sight. As there were two whales, one very large and one much smaller, and as they were playing about the ship all day, the question arose as to the Jonah's for whom they might be waiting. Julia and I were not quite ready to offer ourselves as a willing sacrifice, although I am afraid if the lot were cast it would fall upon us; if I were sure of being landed as happily as Jonah I might not consider it a sacrifice, the experience might not be altogether desirable, but the delight of setting foot on dry land once more would move one to endure, for a short time, much that was disagreeable.

The Cape pigeons have finally left us, they have been gradually falling off for days, yesterday there were two, today we have only three little Carey's chickens to remind us of our large flock of followers.

July 16

Much warmer now, delightful weather, shedding bit by bit my warmer clothing, my thick flannels went some time ago, but even a little flannel is getting to be burdensome, the change is so gradual that one hardly notices it.

July 20

The house-cleaning days have come, days before which those I have heretofore experienced may hide their diminished heads, there are spots out the out-side of a house that some-times escapes the cloth or the brush, but I verily believe there is not a square foot on board ship that is not stowed or tarred or painted or at least scrubbed.

Inside, the reformation began with the sacrifice of the stove that had served us so faithfully, we implored the Captain to defer the day until we were, at least, in sight of San Francisco but no, it was rusty and worn, no amount of blacking would make it clean, in fact it was an eye-sore, as all things not spick and span are to him, and over board it must go. The Captain and I witnessed the final plunge, Axel and the steward were the active agents in the slaughter.

Such an overhauling as we have endured, to keep the rest company I have cleaned my room at least three times. The white paint trim has to be thoroughly scrubbed then painted, the floors stoned, the hard wood in the cabin washed, wiped and polished, the base boards painted brown and brasses polished. When the brass polishing extends to the brasses on the outside shutters of the sky-light and the oiling to the small walnut button that fastens these shutters, one can have an idea of the thoroughness with which everything is done on board ship.

We have been redolent of oil, turpentine, paint and varnish for weeks. We are now only waiting for the tropical rains to devote ourselves to a general clothes scrub, if we were to wash all that we have planned we should not have an article left in our ship's ward-robe. When I left home it seemed to all that I was taking far too much in the line of warm under-clothing, but I can't be too thankful I had it to bring. With care I shall have enough to last me in.

July 21

Eight weeks today since we left Stanley and we are thirteen degrees below the equator. We had set two months as the length of the trip from Stanley to San Francisco, ten weeks at most, and we are ten days from the equator now. The average length of time from fifty degrees S. to San Francisco is fifty three days. The last voyage the Captain went up from the equator in nineteen days but it was in March and now it will be summer, and of course much lighter winds.

The Captain has forbodings also in regard to hurricanes north of the equator and today has been allowing us to realize what a serious matter this is getting to be. Many of the owners are old sea captains and they knowing the condition of our cargo when we went in to the Falklands, also the facilities there to be slight, and that we are coming out in the winter season, knowing all this they will, as the weeks go on, conclude that the ship has foundered off Cape Horn.

There are two rays of hope in all this blackness; the one is that the letters sent the day before we left Stanley and the Captain's vouchers sent a month later, may serve to shorten the time; the letters have probably not yet reached home, so that after receiving them six weeks may elapse before our friends begin to be really anxious. Our other hope is that Captain Whitmore's reputation for exceeding carefulness is so well known the people will feel sure that he will run no risks. Why this voyage should be lengthened so unaccountably is past our finding out, we try always to believe that in some way "it is for the best." We almost conclude that the good people at home are too earnest in praying for gentle winds, we certainly desire their prayers but we wish they would ask for stronger winds.

Since reaching twenty six degrees S. latitude we have been the limit of a strong S.E. trade wind and what do we meet? Varying breezes and dead calms, we hoped and looked forward to making our two hundred miles a day here.

July 22

Still a calm! As Mrs. Whitmore and I were sitting in the door of the after wheel-house, she suddenly cried "A water spout," and sure enough five or six miles away there was a queer, smoky, inverted cone-shaped cloud descending very rapidly towards the water, through a glass we could see the water, as it rose to meet the cloud, whirling about and the

67

spray flying as if it were spinning about a rapidly revolving water wheel set up on end. It was perhaps six minutes from the time we first saw it before it finally disappeared. It was apparently engulfed in the clouds back of it. The Captain came to view the same and said he had never seen nor heard of one being seen in this latitude before. In the Indian Ocean where water spouts most frequently occur, ships are often engulfed, and the only way to break the force of one, is to fire into its center.

Today is the first really warm day we have had, and from this time on we must be prepared to swelter. Julia and I are determined to utter not one word of complaint for when we groaned so over the cold the Captain said he would have us sighing for Cape Horn breezes before we reached California. I think however I shall bear much in the way of heat before I pine for such cold as we had there.

This is just the weather for outside renovation. Tar, slush and paint pots reign supreme and men bespotted with mixtures of blue, red, black and white paint are to be seen swarming up the rigging, tarring the ropes, scraping the masts and yards or suspended in "bo'suns" chairs betwixt heaven and deck painting the chains and braces. All the iron on board ship, the bits, the anchors, and what the unlearned in nautical lore would call chains are painted red. The main wood work, white, and the trimmings, blue, so that, when we are thoroughly in order, I can well believe she will be as neat as a new pin and as fresh as a daisy.

To add to our enjoyment a new moon has come to shed its light upon us, such a slender crescent as it was when we first saw it last evening; it is evidently a very "dry moon" as both horns have a decided upward tendency, and nestled in one corner almost touching it was a tiny star. Mr. Dow encouraged us much by assuring us that a star so near the moon meant wind. One hardly needs a moon in these latitudes, the sky is cloudless and the stars very brilliant, one in particular, the evening star shines with such brightness that long rays are reflected in the water.

July 27

Lovely days and nights, an eight knot breeze, steady for the most part, thermometer standing seventy seven degrees at noon. If were not so anxious for home news how perfectly lovely this would be. School after school of flying fish are about the ship, it is great fun to watch them, but poor things,

68

what is fun for us is death for them, for they rise out of the water only to escape the yawning jaws of shoals of benito for other large fish.

The sailors have caught several benito lately, Mr. Goodwin called us to see a particularly large one today. The benito belongs to the same family as dolphin and is said, in dying, to assume dolphin-like hues; I have never seen a live or dead dolphin but I don't consider the faint shades of magenta marking the sides of the dying benito as brilliant rainbow tints, and it is thus I have always heard the dolphin hues designated in poetry and song.

In the stomach of this benito several flying fish were found, wings and all intact, they evidently eat them "tops and all." The flesh of this fish is considered a great delicacy by the sailors and although they get horribly sick after partaking once or twice, they think themselves abused if they are forbidden to catch any more. Mrs. Whitmore describes the flesh as being very dry and tasteless, and says oftentimes, when there is a full moon or there has been a calm and much heat, it is actually poisonous; indeed it is included in the list of flesh, fish and food forbidden by Moses to the Jews, being a deep water fish and consequently without scales.

The flying fish, on the contrary are very palatable, they are small resembling in size and taste the smaller variety of the Kennebec river smelts. Axel preserved the wings of an unusually large one and presented them to me, they have a much less gauzy appearance after being dried, than when seen glistening and shining in the sunlight, as it bears its owner in its short flight through the air. These little fish resemble nothing so much as tiny birds of exceedingly light, filmy plummage, they only rise for a few seconds then fall with a little splash into the water, sometimes rising again almost immediately.

We have another set of fellow-voyagers now, being accompanied by three or four birds, variously designated "bo'swain," current and marlin-spike bird. Why "bo'swain" I know not, for I have not yet learned a bo'swain's duties; current, the bird flies always against the current in order to seize upon the unwary fish; marlin-spike, because it has a tail unnaturally prolonged, it is such a thin spike that it can only be seen when the bird is directly overhead outlined against the sky, whether it is only one long feather or several folded together I can't decide. The breast and under side of the wings are white and I had supposed it was white all over until I saw one diving for a fish and then discovered that the back and the upper side of the wings were almost black, and the very broad beak was a bright red.

Unlike the Cape pigeons, the current birds do not fly near the ship, nor do they look upon slush as a great delicacy; like nearly all sea birds they have a harsh, melancholy sort of a cry as circling heavily about they fly just above the mast-heads.

July 28

Our lovely breeze continues, but whether, with Mr. Dow, we are to attribute it to the star near the moon, or with Mrs. Whitmore, to the fact that we have been holding, for weeks now, a regular Sunday morning service in the after cabin, its seems difficult to decide, nevertheless we thankfully receive what is given and sail on.

July 30

Crossed the equator in one hundred eighteen degrees fifteen minutes west longitude.

We crossed, this morning, the line which in our imagination divides the northern from the southern hemisphere, and things seem even now to wear a new aspect. The Captain's hatred of the Southern Pacific has influenced even our unbiased minds; personally I have nothing against the region, for it has certainly brought us some of the loveliest weather I have ever known, but now we feel that we are on the last stage of our journey and that San Francisco is indeed our only goal.

We have been out so long that sometimes it strikes me suddenly that I have never known any other life and that it is going on forever. Without realizing if from day to day, there is certainly a great monotony to this life, the days go by and a week has passed, then a month, two months and so the time goes, for notwithstanding the mouthing "tempus fugit," here as fast or faster than on land.

The voyage is always divided into sections, the equator and Cape being the dividing lines. We divide these sections into the smaller portions as marked by degrees, so that now instead of allowing myself to dwell upon the thought of California, I only think of the doldrums and the disagreeable weather to be encountered before we may hope to strike the desired N.E. trade in fifteen degrees west. However as forty days from the equator up is a very long time and twenty four a little more than average I allowed four weeks for the trip, that will take us into San Francisco the very last of August and we expected to arrive there in May. This has been indeed a disappointing trip, but I will not bemoan myself, if only I do not find sad tidings awaiting me in San Francisco.

July 31

We have had a most exciting and delightful day. The morning was [one word], although passed after our usual custom, a bringing out of all sorts of finery stored up for such occasions and adorning our persons with the same, we each try to get something new and startling for Sundays; service in the after cabin at ten, an adjournment on my part to the after wheel-house for the hour before dinner.

I have been so busy all the week that my reading has been behind hand, so had planned to do a good deal today but it happened that I did very little.

At dinner we heard the cry "Sail ho!" and the Captain and I rushed on deck. The "sail" proved to be a sailing vessel but whether ship or bark we could not yet make out as her hull was still below the horizon. In two minutes, the Captain and Mr. Goodwin had decided that she was an American vessel bound south, settled upon her destination, cargo and all about her. I meanwhile was just able to determine her whereabouts through a glass but could no more have told her course than if I had not seen her.

The Captain said we could spend the afternoon signaling her, and ordered new signal arms and halyards, of which he is very proud, to be gotten out and the signals bent on. When we came out after dinner we found the stranger much nearer and could easily make out that she was a full-rigged ship and we thought she had the American ensign flying. We have been so long without direct news from home, we were delighted when Captain Whitmore assured us he would board her if the strange captain were willing to wait, then too our captain was anxious to hear about freights and business generally.

The other captain was evidently anxious that we should report him, for he had already run up his signals, but we could not make out the name. We made our preparations accordingly for an exciting afternoon, we brought out the red cabin chairs and with rugs arranged on one corner of the deck as cozily as possible, looked up and wrote out questions for signaling and had everything in readiness for quick work when once we should begin. With the new arrangement we had only to run the signals as fast as any one could read off the letters;

certain colors and combinations of colors represent certain
letters and a certain combination of letters represent a word
and even a sentence; the signal book teaches us how to com-
bine the two.

Each ship first runs up her ensign, that tells her
nationality; then the letters that represent her name, J. W. M.
V. being the *Berlin*'s; next the letters representing the port
from which she sailed; then those representing the port to
which she is bound; the number of days out; the day's latitude
and longitude. After these preliminary remarks any questions
can be asked and answered, usually one or more in regard to
the wind and weather just experienced, for each is going to
what the other has just come from. On this occasion we had
only to give our name, for the report of our misfortunes has
probably been so wide-spread that it was unnecessary to add
anything.

When we had gotten the stranger's name the Captain
asked if he might send his mate on board, they replied by
backing their yards, the gig was at once ordered out and the
Captain proceeded to give the mate instructions. I would like
so much to have gone, the little boat looked so light and
jaunty and I could have had such an opportunity for seeing our
ship under full sail, but the Captain would not listen to a word
for a moment.

The ship proved to be the *Chas. F. Moody* of New York,
----- Leonard, master, she was built in Bath, Maine, the
same year as the *Berlin*, she is four hundred tons larger than
our ship and carries more sail.

On their first passage the *Moody* and the *Berlin* started
out, one from New York and one from Philadelphia on the
same day and met, four months later at the Golden Gate,
having made the passage, in the same length of time to a day,
and they had not sighted each other once on the voyage. The
captain then in command was an intimate friend of Captain
Whitmore but he is now dead. Captain Leonard is from Bath
or Woolwich, but neither Captain or Mrs. Whitmore have met
him or Mrs. Leonard.

We hastily made a collection of magazines and English
illustrated papers and novels and with a generous slice of the
Stanley birthday cake, offering a prayer at the same time that
the latter might not be the cause of a death in the family, we
sent them off with a note asking for news of the outside world,
of freights, and for a donation of potatoes if they could spare a
few.

There was great excitement in getting and keeping our
ship round where she belonged, for she seemed determined to

bear down and collide with the visitor. After we had seen Mr. Goodwin clamber on board the *Moody* from the small boat, we turned our attention to the deck, scanning then carefully for signs of ladies; after a while two appeared upon the scene and waved to us, we immediately ran up more signals passing all sorts of compliments. The signals are of the brightest red, blue, and orange colors in all sorts of combinations with white and are very ornamental; it is very seldom that I can make out a sentence unaided, but the Captain seems only to have to have a glance through the glass and calls out the letters which we look up in the signal-book.

We consider ourselves very fortunate in seeing so large a ship under full sail, it is the first we have seen since leaving Philadelphia except one on the Atlantic, whose hull did not appear above the horizon.

Before our boat had reached the ship on her return, the *Moody* had squared her yards, dipped her colors, signaled her thanks in return for our "bon voyage" and was well upon her way to the Cape. We seized upon the note that Mr. Goodwin brought us and asked him a dozen questions apiece in two minutes. We learned that Mrs. Leonard, her two children (boys) and a young lady passenger were on board, they had been delighted of the opportunity to send letters back. We also learned that this has been a very disastrous year for shipping, several large ships have been lost, one with friends of the Whitmores in command.

After gaining all the information, in regards to the personal appearance of the ladies, that Mr. Goodwin could give us, we bethought ourselves to ask about potatoes; in the matter of potatoes as well as in every other way, they had been most generous. They sent three large sacks of potatoes, one of onions and one of mixed vegetables (turnips, carrots and beets). Such generosity we had never even imagined. We think now we shall have potatoes enough to last us to San Francisco, and morning, noon, and night we shall bless the name of the donors. So occupied were we with the potatoes that we scarcely heeded Mr. Goodwin's remarks about a basket in the cabin, finally hearing the Captain calling we went down and found a pile of papers, some dating as late as July 6 or 7, half a dozen novels, one or two of the novels being desirable late novels and dearer to our hearts than even the potatoes, a small bag of apples, oranges, four boxes or "tins" of lovely Peak, Freean biscuits, a bag of nuts and three glass cans of homemade preserved fruit. We became so excited over so much richness that we howled louder and louder as each fresh article was drawn from the basket until, at last, the

73

baby scared nearly to death by our outcries, added his voice to the tumult and cried in good earnest. The little fellow really was nearly frightened our of his wits, we finally quieted him and then proceeded to divide the spoils and partake thereof; we are obliged to divide everything in the confectionary lines for Mrs. Whitmore has such a sweet-tooth that she cannot resist nibbling and the first thing Julia and I know we are minus.

If the Leonards could have seen us or heard one half the words expressing our gratitude they would feel themselves more than repaid for their kindness. We are only afraid, that before reaching Liverpool, they will repent sending us such a liberal supply of canned goods, the fruit Mrs. Leonard probably put up herself. We also feel that, if we allow such a slight reminder of the outside world to so upset us as to our minds and bodies (we were quite wild, for a time, with excitement, and Julia had a headache for the rest of the day) we may make up our minds to enter San Francisco raving maniacs.

August 1

These charming, charming days and nights, surely without our attendant cloud of anxiety this would be the height of bliss. The thermometer day after day at noon stands at seventy seven degrees, the sky is cloudless and of a most heavenly blue, a sky peculiar to the tropics, a diffusive not a glaring sunlight (due to the sun's being ahead of us) surrounds us and over a sea of the loveliest aqua-marine tint we are gliding as lightly as a bird, it is happiness to be active and capable of enjoying such richness. The beautiful sunsets that are bestowed upon us night after night are a fitting close for these days and prepare our eyes and our minds for the beauty of the evening.

These sunsets are unlike anything that I have ever seen elsewhere, even in the tropics on the other side, there the tints were so very delicate, here they are not only delicate but with much gorgeous coloring added, not reds but greens, saffron and a ruddy sort of gold; in the Atlantic the sky was either cloudless or with light fleecy clouds, here a bank of clouds extend entirely around the horizon, lighter and of more fantastic shapes in the west. A person of an imaginative turn of mind might see strange pictures in these clouds and one of an artistic or creative mind might attempt a description but such attempts are not for me. Once or twice only has the sun

74

set without its attendent company of clouds, then it dropped a huge ball of fire, not at all dazzling to look upon, into the ocean.

We have seen, in a description of the sunsets in the Pacific, this band of clouds about the horizon mentioned as a distinctive feature of the sunsets of this region, it certainly adds much to the variety of the scene, and it gives us something to look forward too all day, for we are sure to have something new each night, how so many and so very different shades, delicate blues, pinks and grays, and gaudy yellows, oranges, greens and assorted coloring of all sorts, can blend and harmonize as we see this very night, is as always an increasing mystery.

In the evening, after all this splendor we have a moon, which seems to last much longer than moons at home, for we do not lose it for an evening or even for an hour, as there are no storms and consequently no clouds to hide it. We sit out night after night in cotton gowns, without wraps of any description, the air so dry that water spilt on deck even late at night dries up at once, indeed the decks are scrubbed every morning and water used very freely but there is no trace of dampness even when we go on deck before breakfast.

The current birds, which have occasionally visited us before, are with us now in goodly numbers and denote that the easterly current has set in; it is not very pleasing tidings, for this current sets us towards the land, and the greater distance one puts between himself and the North American continent in this quarter and at this season, the more likely is he to escape long doldrums and make a quick passage. We are now in the longitude of San Francisco, further west than the Captain has ever been before, while so far south but he hoped to gain even a few more degrees before falling in with this undesirable assistant. The current extends about 5 degrees of latitude and is running across it. We shall lose probably quite a number of degrees of longitude.

August 2

The dreaded doldrums are upon us I fear, there has been a decided change in the appearance of the sky, the weather is warmer and what would be called a "threatening sky" is all about us. I do not wonder that mariners are weather-wise, with only the sea and sky about them and the winds to study, with careful records of all previous voyages to which to refer, they must become adept in reading the signs and signals of the heavens.

We are really covering degrees of latitude very satisfactorily considering our past ill luck. No one can realize the effect a strong, steady fair wind has upon the feelings of all on board ship, our hearts are light and all our little discomforts shrink into insignificance in the light of the fact that we are getting on. A light or head wind, on the other hand, has a correspondingly depressing effect, the world is stuffed with sawdust on those days. We thought we had become quite resigned to adverse winds and weather but this run of good luck will have spoiled us I fear, for I find myself quite sick at heart as I face the prospect of a long doldrum.

The dipper is gradually appearing, star by star, upon our view and every night we anxiously look and inquire for the north star, thus far nothing has been seen of it; the Southern Cross is slowly sinking lower and lower in the southern sky, but we watch its departure with no feeling of regret.

The Southern Cross, loudly praised and much vaunted has been a great disappointment to us from the first, it is so exactly like half a dozen other crosses in the heavens, that half the time I am not able to find it. I expected to see a cross made up of hundreds of brilliant stars, sparkling in the sky like an immense cross of diamonds and the one object in the whole heavens, before which the other constellations hid their diminished heads. Instead of this dazzling object I find a cross of unequal dimensions, tipped over on its side and made up of four ordinary brilliant stars. Such is life! The one consoling circumstance in this turned about state of affairs in the heavens, is the fact that since we crossed the line the moon has resumed her familiar personal appearance, the old man no longer reposes on his side but sits up with his face as broad and as good natured as ever. Perhaps the further north we get our difficulty in recognizing familiar constellations may lessen and we shall feel more at home with the evening sky.

August 6

The doldrums are indeed upon us and have been for the last four days, the prognostications of the Captain were not in vain. On Wednesday the rains descended and the floods came and we knew we were in for it; it is this horrible wet and dampness in conjunction with the heat and the calm that makes a doldrum in these latitudes so intolerable.

One ray of brightness, in all this gloom, is the fact that water is being stored up by the tank-full and when the rain is over we shall all have a glorious washing day. I can't say I ever before pined to reign over a scrubbing board and tub, but now I look upon wash days as great fun, perhaps if they came oftener I might not enjoy them so much, I have not had a scrub since we left Stanley and now we can have all the water we want.

Another thing that bears our spirits aloft as on wings is the entrancing fact that our breeze has not left us and we continue to make one hundred sixty miles a day. This weather cannot last forever and there is no danger of our being thoroughly mildewed while we are making such strides towards the trade winds and a dryer atmosphere.

I work, work, work from morning till night, being occupied just, at present, with some of the much laughed at piles of cotton cloth that I would persist in bringing. I stitch, stitch by machine and by hand, allowing myself no time to think how uncomfortable I am. I do not even read and only play cards for a little time in the evening, whether owing to the depressing effect of the weather, or to my being thoroughly tired out by night, or for some other good and sufficient reason, I am and have been having, for several nights now, a most horrible run of luck at cards. It is Julia's turn and she is just making up lost games, there is no half way with me, I either win everything or else lose on the same magnificent scale.

Sunday, August 7

The wind died out in the night and this morning we have a bright sun shining and a fine clear atmosphere about us with no sign of dampness.

The very slight breeze, a zephyr fanning our sails, the Captain and mate persist in calling the much desired trade. We certainly have struck something but I can't believe such a light air as this can be even the forerunner of our strong trade wind, however, we are thankful enough to be out of the warm shower-bath-like atmosphere of last week. I rather shudder, though, at the thought of what it will be when we are directly under the sun and no wind, indeed I suppose we may attribute the weakness of the trade (if this is the trade wind) to the near neighborhood of the sun.

This morning we arrayed ourselves in our coolest and whitest garments, mine being a very airy white mull gown at least a thousand years old, but presented by an aunt for just such days and just such weather as this, and at ten we assembled in the after cabin for service.

77

Our congregation is, of all congregations, the most select, all taking a hand at heading the service except the Captain who is well content, to have his places found for him, and to come in strong on the responses.

My part of the service is to read the lessons and one of Phillips Brooks' sermons, usually allowing my audience to select the text, a most obliging clergyman as I try to impress upon my hearers.

We spent the afternoon in the hammock. When not asleep, we took turns reading aloud Black's *White Heather*.

Tonight, after most careful instructions from Mr. Dow, I managed to ferret out the north star and something that was said to be the dipper, what I had been calling the dipper was not it at all, verily I am either losing my eyesight or things are indeed changed. The Southern Cross is no longer visible, it must have disappeared in the clouds of the past few evenings.

Judging from the position of the north star, and to use a nautical expression, we are not "heading up" well. We ought to be making an almost northerly course, for the trade wind gets stronger further north and we want it as soon as possible in all its strength, but with our heavenly guide on out starboard quarter we can't be making much more than a westerly course.

August 8

It is even worse than we expected, for when the Captain got his sight today noon he found that we had made a very poor day's run, only seventy miles in all, and in running that distance, we have made just nineteen miles of "nothing." Seventy miles is a mean day's work, but when reduced to nineteen it is despicable, disheartening in the experience.

This morning I arose with the lark and devoted the greater part of the forenoon to the washing and the afternoon, to the ironing of nearly four dozen pieces. It will detract somewhat from the glory of the achievement, when I add that there were two dozen and a half handkerchiefs, half a dozen towels and as many napkins.

The only excitement of the day has been a full fight, on the main deck, between two of the men. The Captain and first mate, whose watch it was, were in so deep a confab on the poop deck that the contest had become pretty warm, before they realized the men were more than sky-larking. The combatants were separated without difficulty, one of them being Moon, "Moon up in the sky." A pretty hard customer he is too, no sailor, a native of New South Wales, he has probably led a rough life in the mines, all this according to the Captain. I always feel that I must speak a good word in his behalf, ever since he rushed to my rescue (in answer to an agonizing cry) and bore off a flaming lantern that was threatening to burst and spread destruction throughtout my beloved after wheel-house. I deemed it bravery on his part to seize and bear off the blazing mass and he pursued in his efforts until he had extinguished the flames without sacrificing the lantern. If I had dared touch the thing I should have thrown it overboard at once. The Captain did not give him credit for even this valiant deed, but says he did not know enough to know there was any danger.

August 9

The sun today, almost over head, warbled about strangely while the Captain was taking his sight. It seems very warm and yet the thermometer only registered 84 degrees at noon, " but when we get out of this valley" to quote the Captain, "the mercury will run higher and yet it will not seem as warm."

Last night, judging by the north star, even I could see we were heading up much better than the night before and today we find we have made a whole degree of latitude. Also that we have a strong current helping us along, having left the adverse easterly current behind.

We are now in fifteen degrees and some minutes north latitude.

August 11

Paint, paint, paint, nothing but paint from morning till night. Paint pots and brushes on every side, howls of "paint, lookout for paint" if we attempt to set foot on deck; men armed with brushes and besmeared with paint look in at our state-room windows; retire to the cabin and find a man at the sky-light; there are so many hands and they make such quick work that the entire ship is covered with fresh paint. To make the matter worse a fresh wind is blowing and the ship rolls more than she has done for months. Consequently one finds one's self in the middle of the deck with apparently no center of gravity and absolutely nothing to clutch at, the depths of one's woe can only be deepened by being in such a position with the baby clinging about one's neck.

We shall be so very fine, judging from what this first coat has done, when we are all painted up, that we shall be more than compensated for the woes of the present times.

For two days now we have been enjoying the freshest of trade winds, our run today was two hundred miles. The one bitter drop in this cup of bliss being that the stronger the wind gets the farther round to the north it draws. Consequently the ship does not head up to the north as we would like. If we were making latitude only we should be just spinning along, even as it is we are nearly twenty one degrees north latitude and on account of the wind and the overcast sky the Captain thinks we are sure to escape the hurricane he has been rather dreading, it would be quite on the program at this season anywhere under thirty degrees north latitude.

We are in the latitude of Honolulu now and the air seems so much as it does at the sea-shore at home, although we have no fog.

If we only could keep up and gain no more longitude! For west of one hundred thirty degrees W. longitude we are sure to strike head winds and the consequences will be we shall have to run far to the north of San Francisco and work down. We are now very nearly at one hundred thirty degrees W. longitude and a strong wind blowing.

August 15

The trade wind has all day been preparing to take its leave. The sun has been shining clearly and a blue and perfectly cloudless sky. The days of cloud and dampness, the gray days in fact as well as the later strong winds are all things of the past. We are now entering upon the belt of variables and being so far west the Captain fears they will be headwinds. He also thinks that, with a strong, fair breeze he could run us into San Francisco in four days. We shall probably be ten or more.

There being such perfect yachting weather today, I am reminded of Southport and the good people there. I can imagine how the yachts are flying about the bay and the Nasons, Pigeons and others at Captain Gray's making their daily and semi-weekly trips to Squirrel Island and Boothbay.

We are joined today by several birds of the duck, goose and albatross variety; duck as to their color, goose as to their shape and size and albatross as to the beak, and all as to their cry which is a mixture of quack, hiss and scream. These birds rejoice in the intellectual name of "goonies."

The painting still goes on and we are called out on deck a dozen times each day to admire new effects in red, white and blue. The baby manages to get a hand or foot covered with fresh paint at least twice a day and just howls until it is removed evidently considering himself badly injured.

Lovely, lovely sunset tonight, each night we say "surely this is the loveliest of all."

August 16

We are now in the calm belt between the trade wind belt and that of the variables. The ship is not steering, all the morning the water was like a mirror, the goonies floating about us on it, not able to rise, since they require a breeze to aid them in raising their heavy bodies from the water. We spent some time in the wicked pastime of fishing for one of those birds, but they, one and all, declined to partake of a tempting bit of salt-pork offered them on the point of a fish-hook.

I work on, early and late, I do not allow myself an unoccupied moment. I have taken to running the machine and stitch for the family. It is only by planning quantities of work and structuring myself that I manage to bear the delays, now that we are so near our port.

This afternoon a breeze sprang up and the Captain tacked ship. I have seen it done so many times now that it is no novelty, still I am never tired of watching the yards as they slowly come round. I was therefore promptly on deck tonight. Such a bedlam it seemed with the men shouting their shantees in different keys in different languages in different parts of the ship. The wind has been in one direction so long there has been no work at the sails except bracing the yards at night. Consequently the men's lungs have had a rest.

The change in our course brought the sun round to set on the stern tonight. When we came up from supper and saw the change (we had not noticed it until the sun was low) it seemed quite as if the west at home should change places and we should look to the south for our sunsets.

Doldrums, Doldrums, Doldrums. Five whole days of absolute calm, a sea fairly oily in its smoothness, a brilliant sun pouring its rays down upon our devoted heads and our hearts heavy like lead within us. We are so very near and yet so very far. Last Sunday we were confident that today we could say "next Sunday we shall be in San Francisco" and today we feel that we are almost as far from it as then. We have less than nine hundred miles to make and still the days go by and no wind.

Mrs. Whitmore says she has always heard that an east wind had as many lives as a cat and now she is ready to believe it. The S.E. trade must die out before we can hope to strike a variable or south wind to waft us into the belt of the northwest trade, that once reached and all would be well.

We had hoped that the new moon two nights ago would help us out, this time there was no star near, only Venus some distance away rivaling, in her brilliancy the slender crescent. The sunsets during these doldrums have been gorgeous beyond anything we have had, if that were possible. A new shade has appeared or rather different shades of the same color, a beautiful blue gray, seen in the clouds as well as tinging the whole sky, shades similar to those seen on the inside of a finely marked mother-of-pearl oyster shell. If I could only forget how very anxious the people at home must feel I should thoroughly enjoy everything, the weather, the sunsets, the goonies, everything about this life. The table even, with the addition of new potatoes and vegetables (minus the onions) has not yet palled on my taste; it really is wonderful how much more of an appetite I have had since leaving the very cold weather. Mrs. Whitmore predicted that when we were so near our journey's end we should so pine for the flesh-pots of San Francisco in the way of vegetables and fruit, that we should entirely lose our appetites for the ship's stores, but nothing of the kind has occurred. This fact is partly owing to the ingenuity displayed by Mrs. Whitmore in planning new dishes for us and getting up little surprises. She is much concerned over the fact that we are on our last seven pounds of butter, whether it will last us in depends upon the wind, but it looks doubtful. Notwithstanding my good appetite I am losing flesh, much to my disgust, since July 9. My weight has been reduced from one hundred twenty five pounds to one hundred eighteen and I was feeling so proud of my noble proportions.

The hour for our usual Sunday service was changed today

from morning service at eight to a vesper service at four p.m. The volume of Phillips Brooks' sermons, loaned me by Mrs. Stanwood, has been a great comfort to us; we have nearly exhausted its contents now, but the sermons will all bear a second or third reading.

While the rector of the Stanley church was away the Governor conducted the services and he used to fall back on a printed sermon for that portion of the service. I had a mind to offer him this collection in order that his congregation might have the pleasure of listening to one or two thoroughly good sermons.

Nine p.m.--a fresh breeze, which we are in hopes will work round into the longed for N.W. trade. We are now making a nearly northerly course. This pleases me much, as I had predicted a change today.

August 24

Head winds, calms, light variable winds, shifting to an opposite quarter the instant an attempt is made, by tacking ship, to make a little better course. Surely Job's trials were as nothing compared to ours, or if that is sacrilegious, I will put it mildly and say we have been much tried.

To such an extent have we fought, bled and died for every mile we have made since leaving Stanley that the Pacific Ocean may truly be said to be tinged with our heart's blood. Our run to the equator on the Atlantic side was made in twenty eight days, and is the only part of our journey on which anything that strikes of good luck may be said to have attended us.

From the very beginning (our long delay in Philadelphia being the commencement) perhaps I ought not say bad but a baffling sort of luck has followed us. What makes it more trying to us all is the fact that we have allowed ourselves to set a limit to the voyage. Last Sunday we thought it more than safe to say "next Sunday we shall be in California." We have sorted out and packed our trunks preparing to send one home and land almost immediately.

We have packed our books and left ourselves in a generally uncomfortable state, and all to no possible good, for tonight there is no more prospect of our landing in San Francisco than there was two weeks ago.

I allow myself no hope now, I shall merely go on from day to day filling each as full as possible with work and reading and making attempts to govern my temper, for I lose patience constantly. I am thankful there is no prospect of my work giving out, Julia is mourning that she is on her last bit.

August 25, 1887

The disgusted author closes this record. Northern Pacific Ocean. Latitude thirty six degrees four minutes. Longitude one hundred thirty nine degrees eight minutes. Ninety one days from Stanley. Two hundred twenty days from Philadelphia.